POLITICAL CONSCIOUSNESS IN JAMMU REGION 1904-1977

Political Consciousness In Jammu Region 1904-1977

SANDHYA DHAR

ISBN : 978-93-5128-104-7

Price : ₹ 690

First Published, 2015

Published by :

Kalpaz Publications
5, Ansari Road, (Near UBS Publishers Distributors)
Dariyaganj, New Delhi-110002 (India)
Mob. : 9811692060
E-mail: books@gyanbooks.com
For Authors: editor@gyanbooks.com

Laser Typesetting : Shubham Printers, Delhi
Printed at : G. Print Process, Delhi

Cataloging in Publication Data—DK
Courtesy: D.K. Agencies (P) Ltd. <docinfo@dkagencies.com>

Dhar, Sandhya, author.
Political consciousness in Jammu region 1904-1977 / Sandhya Dhar.
pages cm
Includes bibliographical references (pages) and index.
ISBN 9789380222561

1. Jammu (India : Region)—Politics and government—20th century. I. Title.

DDC 954.6 23

Dedicated

to

The Loving

Memories of

My Parents and Brother

Acknowledgements

Greateful to the, J.N.U. Library, Delhi; I.G.N.O.U. Acknowledgements Library. Delhi. Ranbir Library, Jammu Central Library Jammu University; Department Library of History Department; Iqbal Library of Kashmir University. Without their co-operation, it would not have been possible for me to complete this work.

I will always be remain greatful to my father Late Mohan Lal Dhar and Late Sanjay Dhar my brother who have inspired me. Their fond and loving memories will always remain in my heart. It is with their blessings that I have been able to complete this book successfully.

Contents

Preface

Handling of the subject of Political Consciousness in Jammu Region from 1904-1977 was a very challenging task. The challenge was poised not so much by the sequence of events as by the analysis of the origin in nature of the consciousness.

The work on political awakening in Kashmir or the struggle for freedom in Kashmir has been well transcripted but nothing has been written on Jammu's political consciousness or awakening. Only off-hand and tangential remarks on this subject in their writing are found. So conscious of the importance of this subject, I undertook an authentic study of the Political Consciousness in Jammu Region from 1904 AD-1977 AD.

However, collecting information for this study was fraught with many difficulties. One of the serious difficulties was to find the state records which were not available due to one reason or the other. The task was made more difficult by the State Government's ban on the use of unpublished confidential records pertaining to the agitation. These records have not been opened since 1947 onwards.

In addition to this, there exists the problem of getting the records of some *sabhas* (social organisations) for one reason or the other.

However, the work is primarily based on the National Archives records, J&K State Archieves, Jammu. Government Publications, pamphalets, Census Reports, journals, dissertations, newspapers and books.

I would like to express my thanks to the staff of the state Archive of Jammu and Kashmir, Delhi National Archives, New Delhi.

INTRODUCTION

Jammu Region At The Dawn Of The Twenthieth Century

The state of Jammu and Kashmir came into being as a single political entity in 1846 with the treaty of Amritsar on 16th March 1846, between the British India Government and Maharaja Gulab Singh. The three regions Kashmir, Jammu and Laddakh came under the rule of Gulab Singh, the Hindu Dogra Ruler.[1]

The state of Jammu and Kashmir occupies a position of great strategic importance in the north-west of India.[2] It is separated from the rest of the country by mountainous and uneven terrain.[3] A prominent feature of the state is its heterogeneous composition, i.e., geographically, culturally and religion-wise. Geographically, it is divided into four natural divisions. The southern plains, the mountainous region, the middle track of Himalayas and the far-off Himalayan region.[4]

The first region consists of plains bordering the Punjab and the broken mass of the foothills known locally as *Kandi* areas. On account of being its mostly strong and arid, cultivation here is scanty, scattered and wholly dependent on rain. The whole of Jammu district and part of Kathua fall into this region. Rest of the Jammu province, i.e. district of Udhampur, Poonch, Doda, and part of Kathua fall in the outer hill region. It consists of low hills laying roughly to the south of Pir Panchal range which separates two provinces of Jammu and Kashmir. [6] Except in the fertile valleys formed by the river and its tributaries, cultivation is scare and scattered and is done on small patches.[7] The middle-track of Himalayas, the third geographical region of the state is known as the Kashmir valley.[8] The region has a rich alluvial soil and paddy and fruits are the main produces of the region. The rest of the state consists almost entirely of snow-capped mountains, with plateaus and glaciers, rocky river valleys and wastes. [9] At present, it comprises of Kargil and Leh divisions of frontier district of Laddakh. The whole of the area is dry and almost rainless. The cultivation of barley maize and millets is, however, undertaken in this region with the help of irrigation from small canals known as *"Kuhls"* which are fed by melting snow.[10]

Jammu Region

In the beginning of the twentieth century, the state was being ruled by Maharaja Pratap Singh (1885 - 1925 AD) who had succeeded his father, Maharaja Ranbir Singh on 12th September, 1885.[11] Soon after his accession, the relation between the Maharaja and the British Indian Government became strained. In 1889, Lord Lansdowne deprived the Maharaja of his political power on account of false charges of mal-administration.[12] A four-member council headed by Raja Amar Singh, brother of Maharaja Pratap Singh, was constituted to carry on the administration of the State.[13] However, in 1891, Lord Lansdowne paid a visit to Kashmir, and a new Council was constituted with Maharaja Pratap Singh as its President and Raja Amar Singh as Vice-president. Four other members were also nominated to this council.[14] The Council was guided by the advice of the British Resident in Kashmir in all matters of importance.[15] In 1905, the Council was abolished and its powers were restored to Maharaja himself,[16] assisted by the Chief Minister, Raja Amar Singh and ministers in-charge of the Revenue and Judicial and Home Departments.[17] However, the Maharaja's powers, especially in financial matters, were subject to manifold restrictions.

The annual budget had to be prepared in consultation with the British Resident in Kashmir, and to incur expenditure not provided for in the budget, previous approval of the Resident had to be sought. Thus, the Resident exercised full financial control over the state exchequer.[18] However, these restrictions were gradually relaxed and the Maharaja was granted full administrative powers, in March 1921.[19]

In 1901, Jammu region was divided into four districts, Jammu, Udhampur, Bhimber, Jasrota and two main feudatory *Jagirs*, Bhaderwah and Poonch.[20] The rulers of these *Jagirs* were feudatories to the Maharaja and their relationship was defined by Ranbir family code (*Dustur-ul-Amal*), which was revised by Maharaja Pratap Singh on 25th March, 1893.[21] This system continued till 1928 when a revised '*Patta*' was issued to govern the relation between the Maharaja and the Raja of Poonch, according to which the latter was to abide by and follow without demure, the advice and direction of the former in all important matters. During the decade 1901-1911, district Bhimber was abolished and two new districts of Mirpur and Reasi were constituted in its place. Mirpur district included the tehsils of Mirpur, Bhimber and Kotli while the tehsils of Reasi and Rampur-Rajouri constituted the district of Reasi.[23] After partition, the Doda district was carved out of Udhampur district in 1948, with this change Reasi lost its district status and became a tehsil headquarter in Udhampur district. At the same time, Poonch district was carved out from the territories of Poonch jagir and Rampur-Rajouri, which was previously a part of Reasi District. However, in 1968, Rajouri was given the status of district. During the year 2007, the state was again reorganized by creating eight more districts. Of these four are in Kashmir Province and four in Jammu province. In Jammu, the four districts are Samba, Kishtwar, Ramban and Reasi.

Geographical Conditions of Jammu Region, Location, Region and Boundaries

Jammu region, one of the constituents of Jammu and Kashmir state lies between 32°-15' to 33°-30' North Latitude and 74° to 76°-15' East Longitude. [24] The province was surrounded by Chamba and Kangra in the east, by Jhelum district in the west by Gujarat district in the south-west, and Sialkot and Gurdaspur district of the undivided Punjab in the south, while the Pir Panjal separated it from Kashmir, in the north.[25]

Area

In 1901, the area of Jammu province was 12,378 sq miles.[26] After 1947, some parts of Poonch and the major portion of Mirpur district came under the illegal possession of Pakistan, and the area of the province shrank to 10,073.1 sq. miles.[27]

The table, given below, gives the figures of area of Jammu region given in the census Report from 1901 to 1961[28].

Year	*Area in square miles*
1901	5,233
1911	12,439
1921	12,165
1931	12,378
1941	12,378
After partition 1947	10,073.1

(26,079.4 sq kms)

In terms of area, Jammu region was the second largest constituent of the state. Whereas it was larger than Ajmer Marwara state (2,711 sq miles), Alwar (409.5 sq miles), Jaipur (11,459 sq miles), Travancore state (7,625 sq miles) and Cochene (1,480 sq miles). It was smaller than N.W.F (13,518 sq miles) province and Jaisalmer (16,062 sq miles), When compared to other countries of the world, this province was larger than Belgium (1 *1,755* sq. miles) and slightly smaller than Switzerland (15,940 sq. miles).

District-wise Area

As per the figures of the census report of 1931, Udhampur district with an area of 5,070 sq. miles was the largest in the state, including Ladakh district (45,762 sq. miles) and frontier *Ilaquas* (14,680 sq. miles).[30] All other districts of the province, were smaller than the average area per district (2,399 3/8) in the state in 1931.[31] After 1947, Reasi and Mirpur districts were abolished and Doda[32] and Poonch were constituted as new districts, thereafter Doda is the biggest district of the province with an area of 4,380.2 sq miles while the size of Udhampur district was reduced to 1,731.6 sq. miles.

The following statement gives the figures of area of different district of the province in 1961.[34]

District	*Area in square miles in 1961*
Jammu	1,248.6
Kathua	1,023.6
Udhampur	1,731.6
Poonch	1,689.1
Doda	4,380.2

Out of four natural divisions of the state, i.e., (I) The sub-mountain and semi-mountainous tract,(II) the outer hills, (III) the Jhelum valley, and (IV). the Indus valley or Tibetan and semi-Tibetan tracts. Jammu region occupies the first two divisions.[35]

This region is partly plain and partly broken *Kandi* (Parched) land skirting the sub-Himalayan ranges.[36] It comprised the tehsils of Kathua and Jasmargarh, the entire district of Jammu and tehsils of Bhimber and Mirpur.[37] The plain tract is the continuation of the northern plains of India along the northem border of the Punjab. Stretching for more than 150 miles, between the Ravi and the Jhelum, the plain tract extended into this province for about ten miles near Kathua, but around Mirpur the hills were near the border.[38] The average height of this plain tract carried from 1,000 to 1,200 feet. The Ravi, the Chenab and several perennial streams watered this tract.[39] To the north of this plain is parched land. This last portion of the plain tract adjoins the outer hills. It stretches from the Ravi to the Chenab, all along the north of the plain tract. It is land of craggy hills and sugged rocks, a continuation of the Siwalik geological formation rising from the plains of the Punjab to an altitude of 2,000 to 4,000 feet above sea level.[40] The tract is dry due to two reasons *first* the soil is porous, made of lighter loam, thickly strewn with pebbles and boulders and *secondly* the local ravines originating from the low hills, are not snow fed rivers, as such they carry water only in rainy season.[41] The *Kandi* tract forms a gentle slope of excessively stony soil with its innumerable stony ravines, which often spread out and do much damage to the countryside by washing away rich components of the soil during rainy season and expose only stony soil.[42]

Tehsil Basoli of Kathua district, the entire districts of Reasi and Udhampur, tehsil Kotli of Mirpur district (now POK), the whole of Poonch and Bhaderwah jagirs constituted a separate region of Outer hills.[43] This region mostly comprises on low lying hills to the south of the Pirpanjal. The atitude of the greater part of this belt varies from 2,000 feet to 3,000 feet whereas the hills of Bhaderwah reach heights of over 5,000 feet above sea level. The name Siwalik (*Sawa lakh*) was given to these hills because of their number.[44] Ravi, Ujh, Tawi, Chenab, Tawi-Manawar, Punch river and numerous hill torrents drain this tract.[45]

Soil

The flat sub-mountain tract of Jammu region has the soil of tarai lands of the east. It is alluvial in nature varying from loam to sandy loom. Phosphate and potash contents of the soil are fairly good, but nitrogen content is lesser. Being fertile, this plain tract of the province shares the advantages of the Punjab plains. [46]

Arid kandi is compo sed of ferruginous clay intermixed with soil and stone. Parched *kandi* tracts are found in the tehsils of Kathua, Hiranagar, Samba, Akhnoor and in some parts of Jammu and Rajouri. This kind of soil is also found in Bhimber and Mirpur tehsils. Being water bearing horizon found at great depth, 50 to 300 feet, this tract is unsuited for digging wells.[47]

Corresponding to two natural divisions there are two different climatic zones in the region. The plain and *Kandi* tracts experience the tropical heat of the Punjab and here the maximum temperature in 1931, stood at 45.7 centigrade and the minimum at 2.5 centigrade.[48] Other parts of the region situated comparatively on higher elevations in the outer hills, experience sub-tropical temperature. However, along the Pir-Panchal range one experiences the climate of temperate zone of Kashmir.[49] One can enjoy salubrious climate at Bhaderwah, Kishtwar and Poonch.[50] While in Jammu scorching heat is experienced in June.

In Jammu region only Chenab, Ravi and Poonch river are snow fed rivers carrying greater amount of water than the rest of the rivers throughout the year. Other rivers are Ujh, Jhelum and Besanlis Tawi.[51]

Because of geographic determinants, crop pattern in this region differs from region to region. The sub-mountain tract of the region below 2,000 feet, yields all the usual crops of the Punjab, viz., wheat, barley, gram Sarshaf (rape) in Rabi (spring) and maize, millet, pulses, cotton, rice and sugarcane in Kharif (autumn).[52] Most of the land especially in *kandi* and outer hills are *ek fasli* (yielding only a single crop in a year due to lack of artificial irrigation facilities.[53]

Jammu region accounted for more than 53 per cent of the (15,21,307 persons) population of the state in 1901, and 56.60 per cent (15,97,865 persons) in 1911. The rate of increase in the population of the region, during the decade (1901-1911) was 5.3 per cent as against 8.7 percent in the whole state.[54] The cause of low increase of population, in comparison to the whole state, were poor harvests and visitations of plague and malaria in the lower tracts of the region, where these epidemics caused heavy mortality.[55]

In 1901, Muslims constituted 57.78 per cent population of the province and this percentage rose to 59.7 in 1911. Hindus, with their 41.16 per cent population in 1901 and 39.2 percent in 1911, ranked second. The Sikhs constituted the third important community, with their 0.86 per cent population, in 1901 and 1.04 per cent in 1911. The other minor communities, constituting the population of the region, were the Buddhists, Jains and Christians, with 4831,439 and 145 heads, respectively, in 1901, and 452,345 and 672 in 1911.[56]

In 1901, out of population of 10,000 in the province the Muslim numbered 5,762, Hindus 4,116, Sikhs 86, Buddhists 32, Jains three and Christian one. In 1911, the numbers of Muslims 5,966, Hindus 3,921, Sikhs 104, Christians four, Buddhists three and Jains two. From these figures it is quite evident that the Sikhs and Christians were adding to their number rapidly. Both these communities were attracting large number of persons to their fold through proselytisation in spite of the opposition of the orthodox people.

The loss of Hindu population during the decade (1901-1911) was due to frequent visit of epidemics and droughts.[57] The Muslims were mostly concentrated the such areas of the province as were almost free from natural calamities, thereby gaining their numbers. However, high birth rate among the Muslims was also responsible for their increase.

The district-wise percentage of main communities, in 1911 was as under.[58]

District	*Muslims*	*Hindus*	*Sikhs*	*Buddhist*
Jammu	38.7	60.2	1.0	
Jasrota (Kathua)	23.1 .	76.6	0.07	-
Udhampur	39.1	60.6	0.06	0.2
Reasi	60.6	39.1	0.2	-
Mirpur		17.7	0.9	-
Bhaderwah (Jagir)	38.3	61.1	—	-
Poonch (Jagir)	90.5	6.5	20.9	-

Occupation soil exploitation in one form or the other was the most important economic activity of the province. In the beginning of the twentieth century more than three-fourth of the population was exclusively dependent on agriculture and its allied pursuits. Absence of satisfactory means of communication and the hilly terrain of the province retarded the growth of trade and industry. Hence, economically the province compared unfavorably with the Punjab and other parts of northern India.[59]

The following statistics will show the relative importance of the main occupations in the economy of the people of this province.[60]

Year	*Agricul-ture*	*Industry Including Household*	*Comm-erce*	*Profess-ions*	*Other Occupa-tions*
1901	76.0	17.55	2.07	1.76	2.92
1911	80.20	7.26	4.82	1.52	6.20
Varia--tion	+4.50	-10.29 -	+2.75	-0.24	+3.28

It is evident from the above Tables that agriculture, commerce and other occupations were gaining favour, while industry and professions were not at all popular.

Agriculture was mainly followed by the Brahmans, Thakkars, Rajputs, Jats, Labana Sikhs, Gujjars and Gaddis. A Dogra Brahman was more an agriculturist than a priest or a teacher. His activities in these capacities were confined mostly to towns. Mohyal Brahmans showed great enthusiasm for joining the army.[61] Inclination of the Rajputs was towards the military profession, so much so that the superior class of main Rajputs considered it below their dignity to touch the plough. Only the Manhas, Charak, Chib, Bhau, Langeh, Beghal, Rakwal and Thakkar Rajputs cultivated land with their own hands.[62]

Mahajans, Khatris and Aroras constituted the economic elite of the region. Trade and commerce were in their hands some of the best officials of the state were drawn from among the Khatris.[63] Tarkhan, Lohar, Dom, Chamar and Kumhar were the menials of the village community, followed their own hereditary occupations and derived their livelihood mostly from the villagers. Gujjars, Bakarwals, and Gaddis were more pastorals than agriculturists in their way of life.[64]

In the field of education, Jammu region was the most backward regions of India. This was due to the scattered population, which meant long distance between focal points of education and their habitation and very limitated schooling facilities. To achieve the goal of education for all was not an easy task, particularly in a traditional society like the one in the Jammu region where; Pari Patti Gali Taratti; Hol Vage Tubra Khage (meaning education brings his ruins, it is by ploughing that bread can be had).[65] Lack of means of communication the general indifference of the people and very limited schooling facilities.[66] Moreover, female education was altogether neglected expected in a few progressive families, parents were generally opposed to girls education.[67]

In the beginning of the twentieth century the literacy rate was very low. According to the census report of 1921 only 27 persons out of every 1,000 were literate in this region. The proportion of literate among the males of this province in 1921 was 47, while among females it was only four. The proportion of English knowing persons in this region in 1921 was still lower. It was only 4.4 per thousand among males and per thousand among females.[68]

However, during the decade 1921-1931 condition improved considerably and the level of literacy in the province rose to 49 per thousand in 1931. Among males the proportion had gone upto eighty two and among females up to ten per thousand.[69]

The district-wise position of literates in 1931, was an under:[70]

District	Literates per thousand population		*Literates in English per thousand population of*	
	Male	Female	*Male*	*Female*
Jammu District	139	22	21.1	2.8
Kathua District Jasmergrah and Kathua Tehsil	73	5	6.2	0.2
Basohli Tehsil	87	7	9.5	-
Mirpur District Mirpur Bimber Tehsil	83	12	7.8	0.1
Kotli Tehsil	58	7	3.0	0.1
Udhampur District	83	4	7.0	0.1
Reasi District	43	3	1.4	-
Poonch Jagir	56	3	3.7	0.1

By the year 1941, the proportion of literates per thousand of population in this region had risen to seventy four, as against seventy in Kashmir region and thirty one in frontier districts, excluding Gilgit Agency.[71] With the expansion of schools and colleges during the following two decades, particularly after the forties, literacy level region rose up to 14.6 per cent in 1961.[72]

Actually the expansion of education was mainly confined to district and Tehsil towns, while the situation in villages was extremely dismal. This can be visualised from the fact that in 1961 only 10.1 per cent of the rural population of this region was literate, as against 46.3 per cent of the urban population.[73]

The percentage of literates among the rural population of Jammu, Kathua, Doda, Udhampur and Poonch district in 1961, was 13.4, 11.9, 8.5, 8.1 and 7.8 respectively, while the corresponding percentage among the urban population was lower. In hilly areas literacy percentage was obviously lower.[74]

During the period of Ranbir Singh (1857-85, the) number of school in Jammu was 33. At the time of Pratap Singh (1889-1892) much progress had been made in education.[75] Equal education facilities were given to the Hindus and Muslims.[76] In his time in 1907, first college was made in Jammu. Hari Singh also introduced Secondary Education and education for girls.[77]

From 1889-1946 in Jammu, there was only one college, 15 high schools, 43 middle schools, 49 primary schools and four teachers' training schools, etc.[78]

As described above, there was no road fit for wheeled traffic which could link the interior of the region. Sanction to the construction of Jammu-Udhampur cart Road was accorded by 1904-1905.[79] Lining work of Nandini Tunnel, 16 miles this road, was executed in 1910-11.[80] Construction of the Banihal card completed as late as in 1922, to whom we called J.V. (Jehlum valley) tunnel.[81]

The isolation of the province was partly shaken when Jammu-Sialkot, the first railway line in the state commence in 1890. This railway was 16 miles in length owned by the state and worked by the north-western railway authorities under an agreement It was an extension of the north-western railway branch line from Wazirabad through Sialkot.[82]

Leaving aside some plain portion of the province, where there was motor or cart traffic, professional muleteers carried on merchandise on pack-animals in the rest of the province. These professional muleteers used to go as for as Wazirabad (Punjab) with their mules, ponies and donkeys and carried merchandise to their interior of the province.

References

1. Pannikar K.M., Founding of Kashmir State, London, 1930, p. 39.
2. Mountainous State of J & 0K almost centrally located in the continent of Asia, in the neighbourhood of Pamir, the roof the world, is popularly termed as the Jewel Decked crown of India. It is bounded by China in the north-west and Pakistan in the west. It is only in the south that it is linked with rest of Indian union. Projected deep into the heart of Asia, Jammu and Kashmir, a component state of Indian union covers an area of 86,023 Sq Kms. extending from 32°17'N to 37°5'N longitude and 72'40'E to 80030'E latitude. The ceasefire agreement of 1st January, 1949 with Pakistan left 84,112 Sq Kms. of area in control of Pakistan. The areas included Giligat, Skardu, Magafrabed, a large part of Poonch *Jagir*, Mirpur district and its adjoining areas. Sudden aggression China in 1962 captured an area of 41,500 Sq Kms.
3. State of J & K occupies, the sixth place in respect of area and sixteenth in respect of population of India.
4. Gupta, N.S., and Singh Amarjit, *Agricultural Development of states in India: Jammu and Kashmir*, Vol.1, Seema, New Delhi, 1979, p. 12.
5. Average height of this region is about 2,000 ft above sea level. The river Chenab flows through it.
6. A large part of this areas laying between 2,000 to 4,000 feet above sea level. The river Chenab passes through this area also.
7. Gupta, N.S., and Amarjit Singh, op. cit. N. 3, pp. 13-14.
8. The river Jhelum with its tributaries, pursuing a zigzag course, flows through the whole length of Valley, bisecting it into almost two halves. The average height of the Valley is 5,500 feet above sea level, while

mountains surrounding it average 12,000 feet with a dip to about 9,000 feet at Banihal Pass.

9. The Indus is the main river of the region. There are a number of mountains over 2,000 feet in height.

10. Due to its topography and scarcity of cultivable land, the distribution of population is most uneven in the state, i.e., Srinagar, Anantnag, Baramulla and Jammu with about 13.7 per cent of total area, contain about 69 per cent of total population.

11. G.O.I F.D Progs. Nov. 1912, No. 62/Deposit-I: Crown films No. 294 (N A.I.) see Fraser's note regarding the rule of His Highness the Maharaja Sir Pratap Singh.

12. *Ibid*, Saraf, Mulkh Raj, *Jammu and Kashmir Encyclop aedia,* 1846-1946, Urdu, 1946, p. 113.

    Nargis, Narsingh Dass, *Tarikh Dogra Desh*, (Urdu), Jammu, 1967, pp. 698-701.

13. *Ibid*, p. 700.

    Sarat Mulkh Raj, *op. cit.*, p. 113.

    Members of the council were:- Raja Amar Singh (President), Raja Ram Singh (Commander-in-Chief of Army), Rai Bhadur Pandit Suraj Kaul (Revenue Member) and Rai Bhadur Pandit Bhag Ram (Judicial Member).

    (i) G.O.I., F.D. Progs. Nov. 1912, No. 62/Deposit-I: Crown films No. 294;

    (ii) Nargis, *op. cit.*, p. 700.

14. Saraf, Mulkh Raj, op. cit., p. 116.

15. G.O.I., F.D. Progs. Nov. 1904, No. 330/Intl-B.

16. G.O.I., P.D., Progs. Nov. 1912, No. 62/Desposit-I; Crown film No. 294;

    G.O.I., F.P.D., Progs. July 1919, Nos. 70-74/Secret-Int1: Crown film No. 293;

    G.O.I., F.P.D., Progs. March 1921, Nos. 1-17/Secret-I; Crown Film No. 292;

Nove, Arthur, *Thirty Years in Kashmir.* London, 1913, p. 48.

17. I.G.I., 1909, p. 72.

    Sufi, G.M.D., *Kashmir,* Vol. II, 1949, pp. 807, 815.

18. G.O.I., F.P.D., Progs. March 1914, Nos 1-2/Secret-I: Crown film No. 293 (N.A.I.).

19. G.O.I., F.P.D., Progs. March 1921, Nos. 1-17/Secret-I; Crown Film No. 292;

    G.O.I., F.P.D., File No. 180-Pol. (Secret) of 1923, pp. 3-16; Crown film No. 1291.

    Saraf, Mulkh Raj, Op. cit., PP. 117, 148 to 151; Nargis, op. cit, p. 702.

20. *Census 1901*, K. Part 1, p. XII (Introduction), *Ibid*, Part II, p. 1.

21. G.O.I., ED. Progs, Oct. 1902, NOSL 111-115, and GO.I., P.P.D., File No. 289. Provisions of *Dustur-ul-Amal'* revised by Maharaja Prop Singh were, I." Annual tribute of Rs. 233.5 annas. 4 Pices., viz., the amount fixed in Sir Frederick Currie's Robbar, dated the 12 May, 1948, can be claimed by His Highness the Maharaja.

22. G.O.I., P.D., File No. 579-P/Sec of 1936, p. l, and crown Film No. 3(B)P/Sec of 1940, pp 1-3, and crown film No. 288 (N.A.9).

23. Census 1911. K. Part 1. p. 6.

    Census 1931, J&K Part 1. pp. 2. 3.4. *A Report on economic and industrial Survey of the State of Jammu and Kashmir.* 1935, 39, 9. J&K. Pub. p. 2-3.

24. Sharma, Baldev, *"Entomological Survey of Jammu Region,"* unpublished thesis, Jammu University, Deptt. of Bio - Science, 1975, p. 9.

25. See Map, *Census 1931*, K. Part-I.

26. *Ibid.*, p. 6.

27. *Census 1961*, Vol. VI, J&K, Part IX, p. 36. *Ibid*, Vol. VI, J&K Part I-A (i), p. 150.
28. *Census 1901* K. Part. 1, p. I; *Census 1911* K. Part 1, p. II; *Census 1921* K, Part 1, p. 4; *Census 1931* K, Part 1, p. 7; *Census 1941* K, Part 1, p. 72.

    Census 1961, Vol. VI, J & K, Part IX, p. 36.

    The figures of areas, taken from the census of 1901 are not reliable as these were based on Drew's estimate in Jammu and Kashmir territories, 1875. No survey had been conducted in the beginning of twentieth century and even the settlement operations were in their preliminary stage, to arrive at the correct figures of area. In the census of 1911, the superintendent in-charge made strenuous efforts to arrive at the correct figures of area. His estimate was based on the information supplied by the survey of India. Thus, he achieved partial success. The figures of area in the census of 1921 were again obtained from the survey of India, but the estimate was not wholly reliable because of the incomplete information with regard to Udhampur district. Only the census of 1931 gives the correct information of area which was based on the correct estimates, supplied by the survey Department of India (Census 1931, J & K Part I, P. 7).
29. *Census 1931*, J & K Part I, p. 7.
30. *Ibid.*, p. 7.
31. *Ibid.*, p. 10.
32. *Census 1961*, Vol. VI. VI, J & K Part I-A (i), D 150; Saraf, Mulkh Raj, *Jammu and Kashmir Guids*, 1969, p. 31. After the tribal raids in 1947 the tehsils of Bagh and Pleadari, some parts of tehsils Handi, Mendhar, Rajouri and Major portion of Mirpur district fell on the other side of ceasefire line. This necessitated for the territorial readjustment of districts, Poonch, a feudatory Jagir under the sovereignty of Maharaja of Jammu and

Kashmir upto 1947, was constituted of full-fledged district with residual portions of tehsil Haveli, Mendhar, Rajouri and parts of Kotli tehsil, left on this side of ceasefire line tehsil Reasi was transferred to Udhampur district and Doda was created a separate district, tabbing Bhaderwah Doda,

Kishtwar and Ramban tehsils of Udhampur district.

33. *Census 1961*, Vol. VI, J & K Part I-A (i), p,147.

34. *Ibid.*

35. *Census 1921*, K. Part I, p. 2.

Census 1931, J&K Part I, pp. 2, 3, 4. *Report on Economic and Industrial Survey of the State of Jammu and Kashmir* 1938-39, G. J & K, Pub., pp. 2-3.

36. Census 1931, J&K Part I, p. 2. *A handbook of Jammu and Kashmir State*, 1945, G. J & K Pub., p. 1.

37. *Census 1921*, K. Part I, p. 2.

38. Randhawa, M.S., *Framers of India*, Vol. I, 1959, p. 198, and Bose, S.C., *Geopgraphy of the Himalayas*, 1972, p. 125.

39. Douie, Sir James, *The Punjab, North-West Frontier Province and 14 Kashmir* 1916, p.3D and Adm. Report., 1997-98 (1940-41 A.D.), p. 2.

40. Census 196l, *Vol.* Part VI, No. 21, p. 1 and *Confidential Gazetteer of Kashmir and Laddakh*, 1980, reprint 1974 pp. 287-288 and Randhawa, M.S, op. cit, p.198.

41. I.G.I, 1909, p. 41.

42. *Review of the Assessment report of the Kandhi tract of Jammu Tehsil*, S. 1981. p. 3.

43. *Census 1921*, K. Part I, p. 2; *Census 1931*, J&K Part I, p. 3.

44. Adm. Report So 1996-97 (193-40A. D), p. 2, and Ganga Nath. p. 19 and *A handbook of Jammu and Kashmir State*, G., J & K Pub., 1945,

45. Koul. Pt. Anand, *Geography of Jammu and Kashmir*, Calcutta, 1913, p. 5.

46. *Census 1911*, K. Part I, p. 12; *Census 1961*, Vol. VI, J&K, Part 1 A(i), p. 189. Singh, Proof. R.L., op.cit.
47. I.G.I., 1909, p. 41 and Ganga Nath, p. 283.
48. *Census 1931*, Vol. VI, J & K, Part l-A (i),p. 2.
49. *Report of the Agricultural census 1970-71*, Vol. I, p. 11.
50. *Census 1961*, Vol. VI, J&K, Part VI. No. 17, p. 3 and *A Hand Book of Jammu and Kashmir State*, 1945, p .3
51. *Punjab State Gazetteers*, Vol. XXII, *A Chamba State*, 1904, p.11.
52. I.G.I., 1909 p. 40, *census 1911*, K. Part 1, p. 12, and Koul, Pt. Anand op. cit., p. 8.
53. G.O.I., ED. Progs. April 1900, NOS. 1-35/Intl- I.
54. *Census 1901*, K. Part II, p. 7; *Census 1911*, K. Part II, p. 2; *Census 1921*, K. Part I, p. 35.

    Figures of percentage have been worked out on the basis of census data of 1901 and 1911.
55. *Census 1931*, J & K, Part 1, pp. 20-21.

    G.O.I., F.D.Progs. Nov. 1902 Nos. 1-21 Intl./B.
56. *Census 1901*, K. Part I, p. 34 and Part II Tab. VI, pp. 2, and *census 1911* K, Part-I, pp. 88-107, and Adm. Report J&K, S. 1968, P. I. (Figures of percentage worked out on the basis of census data).
57. *Census 1911*, K. Part I, pp. 96-108. *Census 1921*, K. Part I, pp. 66-67.
58. *Census 1911*, K. Part I, p. 88. Adm. Report J & K, S. 1968, p. l.
59. *Census 1901*, K. Part I, p. 104. *Census 1911*, K. Part I, p. 226.
60. Figures of percentage calculated on the basis of census data of 1901 and 1911. For detail see *Census 1901*, op. cit., pp 104-108 and *Census 1911*, op. cit., p. 243.
61. *Census 1901*, K. Part I, p. 80. *Census 1911*, K. Part I, p. 201.

62. Binglay, Capt. A.H., Dogras, 1899, pp. 18-25, and I.G.I, Vol. XV, 1908, pp. 99-102.

    Assessment report: Kandhi Tract of Jammu Tehsil, S. 1981, p. 21, and Kotli Tehsil, 1904, pp. 16-19, and Sarna Tehsil, 1914, p. 27, and Ranbir Singh Pur a Tehsil, 1916, p. 19.

63. I.G.I, Vol. XV, 1908, p. 99.
64. *Assessment Reports: Reasi Tehsil,* 1908, pp. 8-43., *and Ramnagar Tehsil,* 1912, pp. 12-13, and Census 1911, K. Part I, pp. 201 - 208, and I.G.I, 1909, pp. 33-34.
65. S.C. Sharma, *"Maharaja Hari Singh-Pioner of Adult Education in Jammu and Kashmir" in Journalism of Social Sciences.* Vol. XIV, University of Jammu, 1997, pp. 103-104.
66. Sharp, H., *A Note on Education in State of Jammu and Kashmir* Calcutta, 1916, p. 2. (Jammu Archive Library).
67. Sharp, H., op. cit., p. 2.
68. *Census 1921*, K. Part I, p. 120.
69. *Census 1931*, J&K, Part I, p. 269.
70. *Ibid*, pp. 269-271.
71. Administration report second half of S. 1998 and S. 1999 (194-43 A.D.) p. 13, and *A Hand Book of Jammu and Kashmir* State, G. J & K, Pol. Dept, 1945, p. 12.
72. *Ibid.*
73. *Ibid.*
74. *Ibid.*
75. *Ibid.*
76. *Ibid.*
77. Seru, S.L., *History and Growth of education in Jammu and Kashmir*, 1872-1973 A.D. pp. 110-135.
78. *Ibid.*

79. I.G.I., 1909, p. 71 and Adm. Report, p.W.D., J&K, S. 1960 (1903-04 A.D.), p. 3 and Adm. Report, Udhampur Tehsil, 1911, p. 5.
80. G.O.I, F.D., Progs, March 1912, Nos. 10-II/Int I-A, p. 9.
81. G. J&K, O.E.R. File No. 654/RR.B-20 of 1920, p. 1, and *Census 1931*, J & K, Part I, p. 14.
82. G. J&K, O.E.R. File. No. 134/R of 1921, p. 21, and I.G.I., 1909, p. 71.

1

ADVENT OF POLITICAL CONSCIOUSNESS, 1904-1931

Political consciousness means a community's awareness of their collective interests and rights. It is acquired through a variety of ways. The political consciousness in India was not the result of a few agitators but it was the revival of historical traditions and popular will of liberation. Several factors contributed towards its growth, e.g., the unification of India, the war's of independence which were fought on the foreign soil, improvement in the means of transport and communication, economic exploitation of India by Britain, racial discrimination which was reflected in inter-personal behaviour as well as the exclusion of Indians from superior administrative positions, English education and the revival of India's past glories.

In Jammu and Kashmir state, political consciousness which became the basis of struggle for democracy was partly a result of the spread of English education, awareness through newspapers, improved means of communication and above all the feelings that they were being exploited and denied their rights by the privileged outsiders.

During the year 1878-79, when Kashmir was hit by a severe famine, it was realised that there was no good road connecting the state with Punjab so that the suffering of the people could have been considerably minimised. This realisation was given a practical shape in 1881, when the construction of a cart road from Baramulla to Kohala was commenced. The road popularly known as Jhelum Valley Cart Road was opened to traffic in 1889. A bridge at Kohala linked Kashmir with British India. The construction of the Jhelum-Banihal Cart Road was another landmark of Raja Partap Singh's rule. Its importance lies in the fact that it connected Srinagar, the summer capital of the state with Jammu, the winter capital, the latter was, however, linked with British India through a railway line in 1890. Based on these principal arteries of traffic, there was also a network of small roads connecting the important towns of the state. These developments had a far reaching consequences, firstly the opening of the Jehlum Valley Cart Road helped in diminishing the old isolation of the valley from outside influence. The improved communication made the trips of British officials, tourists and missionaries more frequent. So, with the opening up of the country by improved means of communications, not only the brisk trade was established between the Jammu and Kashmir and the British Indian provinces, but also it ushered in new ideas and concept of political consciousness in the state.[1]

The twentieth Century ushered a new era in the Jammu region. Virtually, the region remained isolated from the national politics till the beginning of this century. Though some individuals were active in political activities, but majority of the population remained aloof from the political activities, because they considered that the Maharaja belonged to their clan so they should not raise any protest against his rule.[2] So far as the political consciousness in Jammu is concerned it goes back to 1904, when two great Dogra* rulers Lala Hans Raj Mahajan and his associate Sahibzada Hazart Shah laid the foundation of Dogra Committee which later changed its names "Dogra Sadhar

Sabha", a socio-political organisation of the state. The Sabha initiated a programme to eradicate social vices from the society, development of education and protest for the rights of the people of the state. In the nineteenth century, certain administrative measures were western education, transport and communication, printing press, etc. took but on the whole life moved in the old channels in the old way because people of Jammu accepted the Maharaja's administration as he belonged to their community.[4] Their demands were very limited and fulfilled by Maharaja more or less. So, the average Jammuites had no visible reason to feel exploited because the ruling family and most of senior officials came from Jammu which was the seat of power.[5]

The ethno-cultural links with the ruling family made them ignore their exploitations at the hands of the government whereas Kashmiri Muslims believed that their ethno-culture was responsible for their exploitation. The Muslims of Jammu region and especially Gujjars and Bakarwals had their obvious sense of separate identity and interest as compared to that of Kashmir and urban Jammu Hindus.[6] Being educationally and economically backward, they did not react to any political development in the state. The people of Jammu did not show much enthusiasm towards the political struggle of Kashmir started by the educated youth of Kashmir, because the political aspirations of the people of Jammu were alltogether different from those of Kashmir. The people of Jammu identified themselves with the ruler and did not feel any justification of a movement against the Dogra ruler. The most privileged and articulated Dogra people were already placed in a position of power and hence did not share the grievances of the emerging educated leadership of Kashmir.[7] It was also noted that a substantial numbers of Dogra youth were adjusted in the armed forces.[8] Hence, the Dogra masses in Jammu while not getting any direct benefit were psychologically sharing a sense of pride for being a part of the Dogra rule.[9]

Factors of Consciousness in the Jammu Region from 1904-1931

1. Socio-religious reform movements in Jammu region : The socio-religious reform movements were a necessary prelude to the political consciousness in the country.[10] The last decade of the nineteenth century gave birth to a number of socio-religious reform movements in Jammu region, which inculated a sense of consciousness among different segments of the society. These socio-religious movements not only prevailed on the government for the upliftment of their communities, but established their own institutions to spread education, and eradicate social vices from their social fabric.[11] These movements roused in people a sense of leadership and self-assertion for a status of equality in the society, economy and political system.[12]

In the beginning of twentieth century, in Jammu region, a number of socio-religious organisations were formed by different communities. Their aim was to bring some reforms in the lives of people and to make them conscious about their rights and privileges.[13]

2. ***Arya Samaj :*** The nineteenth century India was dominated by the interaction of two civilisations, the Indo-Muslim and the western as introduced by the Britishers. A multiplicity of social, religious and intellectual movements grew out of this interaction and among them the Arya Samaj was the most significant.[14]

The Arya Samaj was founded in 1875 by a vedic scholar Swami Dayanand. The organisation embodied a constructive protest against traditional Hinduism and was theistic in its teachings. In 1877, Swami Dayanand arrived at Lahore at the invitation of the educated Punjabis and Bengalee resident of the locality. During his fifteen months stay in Punjab, Dayanand founded a number of branches of Arya Samaj throughout the province.

His vision of Hinduism, based on the infallibility of the vedas, shorn of polytheism, Brahaminical domination idolatay, and the intricacies of the caste system found ready acceptance among the educated Punjabi Hindus. The Samaj's slogan *"Back to the Vedas"* rightly interpreted proved that those who were inspired to write them were acquainted with the highest truth, which even modern science was yet to re-discover.[15]

On the occasion of the Delhi Darbar, 1877, Swami Dayanand organised a *sammelan* in Delhi to attract the attention of the rulers of the princely states. It was during this meeting that Maharaja Ranbir Singh, the then ruler of the state, came in contact with him. The Maharaja wanted to invite him to his state but the idea was vehemently opposed by the orthodox section of Hindus.[16]

Although, Dayanand personally never came to Jammu and Kashmir, his message reached the state through thousands of traders and state government employees who were mostly Punjabis. The proximity of Jammu to that of the Punjab also helped spread of his movement in this state.

A branch of the Arya Samaj established in 1891 at Jammu was the first one in this area. The road on which its office was located has now been named *"Arya Samaj Dayanand Marg"*. The founding members of this samaj were mostly Punjabi in the state services and some of them carried their private business. Another branch of the *Samaj* originally called Nagar Samaj, was established at Jammu in 1895. It is now called, *"Arya Samaj Purani Mandi Jammu"*. By the end of the twenties Arya Samaj had established its branches at Mirpur, Kotli, Bhimber, Rajouri, Nowshera, Reasi, Ramban, Bhaderwah and Kishtwar.

However, the movement based on monotheism and infallibility of the vedas and shorn of Brahminical domination and rigid caste system was acceptable alike to the enlightened Hindus who desired greater freedom and to the uneducated under-dogs who suffered under the traditional order.[17]

The proselytisation progamme of the Arya Samaj was carried out mainly by a branch of the Arya Pratinidhi Sabha known as the Shuddhi Sabha. The resident was also given to understand that the Samaj had been very active in the Jammu region.

However, the opposition not withstanding, the movement gathered momentum. Beginning from 79 persons in 1901, the number of the Arya Samajists rose to 1,047 in 1911, 23,116 in 1921, 93,944 in 1931 and 87,356 in 1941. The fall in their number, in 1941, was due to the fact that in 1941, a conference of Harijans was convened by the Arya Samaj at Kheri village in Jammu district. There, it was declared that the Harijans were part and parcel of the Hindu society and therefore, they should get themselves registered as Hindu in the census of 1941. It was accepted because of the growing numerical and political strength of the Muslims.

In social life, Arya Samaj tried to raise the age limit for marriage and also propagated widow marriage. As a result, in Jammu province numerous widow marriages were arranged by different branches of the Arya Samaj at different places.

The Arya Samaj was also the most potent force in the state for spread of education among the masses. The work of the Samaj in this field began after the death of Swami Dayanand. In 1883, the leaders of the organisation felt that the prevailing system of education was not suitable to their national needs. A new system of education wedded to the ancient ideals and traditions was according to them, the only answer to the growing problem.

Therefore, the Arya Samaj made education the chief plank of its programme of reforms. In Jammu province, it opened *pathshalas* for depressed classes at Rehari Mohalla, Jammu, Ranbir Singh Pura in Jammu district and Rejog, Chchi, Bhuani, Mengladevi and Kangri in Mirpur and Rajouri districts, at Garh Andral and Kalkar in Kathua district.

The Arya Samaj held female education as one of its cherished objectives. Therefore, a number of Arya Kanya schools and pathshalas were opened in Jammu, Udhampur, Akhnoor and Mirpur. Except for Arya Kanya Pathshala Mirpur, which is now in Pakistan-occupied part of the province, all these institutions are flourishing in the state. The efforts of the movement bore fruit.

The following Table is self-explainatory that in 1931 the Arya's excelled over all religious groups in female education in various age groups.[18]

Religion	*Arya Groups*			
	5-10	10-15	15-20	20 & above
Hindus	262	192	108	55
Aryas	476	382	279	163
Muslims	134	105	64	36
Sikhs	357	297	221	124

It also played an important role in the political field and created national consciousness in Jammu region.

It created community consciousness[19] among the masses of Jammu region through its proselytisation and Shudhi programme (Purification). It not only tried to keep the depressed classes within the fold of Hinduism but also tried to absorb in those who had embraced Islam or Christianity.[20] Arya Samaj called the people to meet in sammelans, organised public meetings and took out processions.[21] They appealed the students to give up colleges, and doctors and lawyers to renounce their services for the cause of *swaraj.*[22] The samaj became in some cases "entirely of an extremist political character." It enrolled membership from the non offical clerks and teachers as well as many high officials of the state.[23]

Its leader in Jammu preached in fovour of non-co-operation including boy-cotting, schools and renouncing of government files. They also propagated the political programmer Mahatma Gandhi in the light of which the samjists appealed to students to give up colleges and doctors and lowyers to renounce their services for the cause of the swaraj Lectures an political themes such as "how develivers.

3. ***The Guru Singh Sabha :*** The earlier Sikh movements of the Nirankaris and Namdharies had failed to respond to the challenges of the time. On the other hand, the efforts of Christian and Arya Samaj missionaries to win over the Sikhs to their respective fold had alarmed the orthodox Sikhs. However, the Sikh community itself was divided into two groups, one who considered Sikhism as a new faith with an independent entity and the other who considered Sikhism as a branch of the Hindu[23] protest movement still owing allegiance to the Hindu deities and connection.[24]

In such circumstances, the need was felt to save the Sikhism from being absorbed in other faiths. Consequently, in 1873, an organisation called Sri Guru Singh Sabha came into existence. The Sabha became popular and by 1879, numerous Singh Sabhas sprang into existence in different party of Punjab. Obviously, the Singh Sabha became a religious reform movement among the Sikhs not only in Punjab but also in J&K state.

However, a branch of Guru Singh Sabha was established at Jammu in 1893. Since a fair proportion of the Sikh population was concentrated in the western part of the state particularly in Mirpur and Muzaffarabad district, the Guru Singh Sabha were established in *samvat*

1963 (1905-06) at both the district headquarters. The aims and objectives of these Sri Guru Singh Sabha, were the same as in Punjab, viz., renaissance of Sikhism by preaching the spiritual massage of the gurus, production of religious literature in Punjabi language, campaign against illiteracy and carrying on proselytising activities.[25]

However, the need of a central organisation was felt to organise the various units of the Singh Sabha, that had sprung up all over the country to concentrate their energies, and to guide and control their activities. Efforts towards this direction were made by S. Sunder Singh Majithia. A big Dewan was held in Maulvi Bangh Amritsar on 30th October, 1902. After an *ardas* of inception by Bhai Teja Singh Bahadur, by laws of the Dewan were firmly adopted. Thus, the Chief Khalsa Dewan was registered under the Act XXI of 1861. All the Singh Sabhas, Khalsa Dewans and other Sikh societies were now affiliated to the chief Khalsa Dewan.[26]

The chief Khalsa Dewan not only brought all the Singh Sabhas under one organisation, but it also acted as a sabhas evoking source of inspiration for the Sikhs outside Punjab.[27] It also acted as a watchdog for the protection of their social, political, economic and religious interest.

Since the advent of Sikhism in Jammu and Kashmir state a number of Gurudwaras had been established. In almost every village, these Gurudwaras were useful in introducing social reforms regarding elimination of caste distinctions and the *pardha* system. They also discouraged child marriage among the Sikhs, even before 1929 when the Infant Marriage Act was passed.[28]

One of the main plank of Chief Khalsa Dewan was to educate the Sikh masses. With this end in view, the office of the Educational Committee of the Chief Khalsa Dewan was brought to Majithia House, Amritsar. The first session of the Sikh Educational Conference was held at Gujranwala with Sardar Bhagat Singh, i.e., Rais of Kula (Lahore) in the chart. It made apoint to establish a school or college at a place where its meeting would be held.[29]

Following the footsteps of the Chief Khalsa Dewan, the Sikhs of Muzaffarabad established a primary school in 1890. This was the first school of its kind in the state. Similarly, the Singh Sabha Jammu, under the able guidance of Jiwan Mukta established a Gurmat Kanya Pathshala. In 1901, it was raised to middle standard. The Singh Sabha Mirpur, also ran a girl's school at Mirpur.[30]

On April 13, 1918, in connection with the Baisakhi Gurupurb, the Khalsa Youngman's Association held a big Dewan in the temple of *Dewan Jawala Sahai* (popularly known as Dewana Mandir), Jammu. It was resolved that special scholarships may be granted to the Sikhs of the state, who were poor and backward, and teachers to teach 'Gurmukh' (Punjabi) in the state schools should be appointed on the Punjab pattern.[31]

In response to the Sikh demands, the state government not only earmarked an amount of Rs. 2,308 for scholarships, exclusively for the Sikh students but it also appointed Punjabi teachers in government schools. It also promised that as soon as their funds increase, they will appoint more Gurumukhi teachers and would be provided for those schools where the number of Sikh students would justify such appointments.[32]

By 1931, the Sikhs had occupied the topmost position both in male and female literacy, having 210 male and 37 females in a thousand of the population in each sex.[33] Confining attention to make more literates one finds that in Jammu district, Sikhs had more literates than Hindus or Muslim. The same was true in case of Kathua and Mirpur districts, excepting Kotli tehsil where Hindus claimed higher literates than Sikhs. In all other districts of Jammu region, the Sikhs had more literates against other communities for the district of Kashmir province, the Hindus were invariably more advanced than the Sikhs.[34]

4. Anjuman-Islamia Jammu : This organisation was the oldest organisation of Muslims in Jammu and was founded in 1893.[35] It was founded by Raja Farman Ali Khan, Major General Samander Khan Chowdhary, Gulam Abbas and Mistri Yaquab Ali. Its mission was to protect the rights of the Muslim subjects to work for their educational advancement, to improve their economic conditions and to free from social evils. Public meetings were organised by the Anjuman from time to time.[37] Their main aim was to beware the Muslim masses about their backwardness for decades under the state government.[38] It extended its activities to Ramnagar, Basohli, Kishtwar, etc.[39] Later, its branches were also established at Kathua, in April 1922, at Mirpur in January 1923 and in Kotli, in June 1923.[40]

It was semi-political body. It believed in constitutional methods for solving the problems and it always pursued the "Policy of Moderation in fighting for its ends.[41]

It played an important role in spreading education among the Muslims of Jammu and number of schools for boys and girls were opened in this region.[42] An orphanage and a boarding house too were also run by the Anjuman out of their own funds.[43]

With the spread of education the Muslims became more and more conscious about their rights, i.e. political and social.[44]

5. The Anjuman-Ahl-i-Sunnat-ul Jammat and Anjuman Ahl-i-Shaia : The Muslims of this region had also formed two other organisations, i.e. the Anjuman-Ahl-i-Sunnat-ul Jammat in 1904 and Anjuman Ahl-i-Shaia. The headquarters of both these organisations were at Jammu. The objectives of both of these were religious preaching, spread of education and helping the orphans.[45]

6. Dogra Sadar Sabha : Dogra Sadar Sabha, is one of the oldest social organisations. It was established in 1904 by Lala Hans Raj Mahajan and his associate, Sahibzada Hazarat Shah. Its earlier name was Dogra committee, which was changed to Dogra Sadar Sabha in Jammu in 1904.[46]

Its main aims and objectives were:

1. To strengthen social and cultural unity by promoting mutual co-operation and goodwill among different segments of the people of the state.
2. Peaceful persuasion of the government to accede to the genuine demands of the people.
3. Struggle for social, cultural and economic development of the state.[47]
4. Rousing social and political consciousness among the people.
5. Bringing to the notice of the authorities, the wrong action and politics of the governments.[48]
6. Pressurising the state government for the spread of education.
7. Struggling for granting more and more rights to the permanent residents of the state.

Activities of the Sabha : Dogra Sadar Sabha had played an important part both in social and political fields. Previously, there was a ban on the press and the platform in the Jammu and Kashmir state but after the formation of Dogra Sabha and with the strong determination of Lala Hans Raj the ban was removed and he succeeded in getting the permission to start the newspaper *Dogra Gazette* in 1905.[49] To give wide publicity to its programmes and policies and to bring into notice of the government the demands of the people, the Sadar Sabha started publications through periodicals and *Dogra Gazette* in 1907. Their periodicals had considerable affect on the minds of the people and also awakened them socially and politically.[50] Dogra Sabha helped to eradicate mass illiteracy among the people and passed resolution from time to time, to impart free and compulsory primary education and to open colleges, high schools and technical institutions. It also voiced for the right of elections for the Harijans and of granting liberal scholarships to students.[51]

The major problem to which the Sabha devoted its attention was the protection of the rights of *state subject* in the services. Because Dogra Sadar Sabha claimed that many outsiders were employed not only in the government jobs but trade and industries were also in their hands. It was the first organisation which demanded that preference should be given to state subjects and not to the outsiders, those who were in government jobs, Trade and industries.[52]

Beside the social activities, the Dogra Sadar Sabha taking part in the political affairs also during the reign of Maharaj Hari singh. It favoured the activities of Indian National Congress in freedom movement. Sabha was also in favour of *swadeshi* movement and propagated the use of *khaddar* and fought against the use of foreign goods. In 1930, when Gandhi ji gave a call against foreign goods, it was Dogra Sadar Sabha, which organised a "*Holi*" of foeign goods or clothes near Purani Mandi in front of city thana at Jammu.[53] The voice of the Dogra Sadar Sabha was so strong that the government passed a law regarding *'state subject' in April 1927.*[54]

For taking active part in politics and administrations, Mr G.E.C. wakefield ordered the Maharaja to declare a ban on Dogra Sadar Sabha on 9th May, 1930, because of its being unlawful body.[54] The ban was removed on the birthday ceremony of Maharaj Hari Singh on 31st October 1931.[55]

In the early thirties, the Dogra Sadar Sabha raised a strong voice for the establishment of a popular assembly in the state[56] and in 1934 an assembly called Praja Sabha was constituted.[57] After 1947, Dogra Sadar Sabha became more active organisation and took part in the political affairs of the state.[58]

Since 1953, it participated actively in the deliberation of the National Conference. It worked not only for the people of Jammu region but for the whole of the state and introduced a number of reforms for the welfare of the state.[59]

*7. **Rama Krishna Sewa Ashram :*** In early 1909, Rama Krishna Sewa Ashram, a Hindu organisation played an important role in Jammu. Its effect was on the well-educated section of the society.[60]

With these organisations little radical changes took birth in the behaviour of the people in urban areas and people became conscious of their rights.

*8. **Young Men's Muslim Association :*** The Young Men's Muslim Association, Jammu was formed towards the close of 1920's.[61] In this year Anjumans were divided into two groups because of frictions among them. Its aim, too, were the same, i.e. to spread education among the Muslims[62], foster spirits of co-operation, to persuade the Muslims to give up bad social customs and to help the poor and needy persons.[63]

However in 1931, it took part in the political affairs of the state and converted itself into a full-fledged political organisation. It gave birth to the young cadres and trained workers those who worked for mulims.[64] It became a platform for the communal Muslim leaders like Chowdhary Gulam Abbas, Gohar Abdul Rehman and others who played important role in 1931 agitations.[65]

2. Education

In the field of education, Jammu region was one of the

most backward region of India because people were socially conservative and conditions were more distressing than in many other parts of country.

Before 1889, education in this region was mainly primitive and manned by religious bodies[66] but by the end of nineteenth century, western education was introduced. The first high school in the state was opened in Jammu in 1890 and the first college was opened in 1907 in Jammu known as Prince of Wales College.[67] According to census of 1931, the condition improved considerably and the level of literacy in the region rose to 49 per thousand.[68] Among the males, the ratio had gone upto 82 and among female to ten per thousand.[69]

It is clear from the above facts that the development of education and thought created a sense of class awareness among the people and they became conscious of their rights and privileges.[70] The minds of the young men filled with the ideas of western political thought, freedom and equality demanded that only the people of Jammu and Kashmir be employed in the administration of the state and government jobs given to them, not to the Punjabis.[71] This gave rise to the protection of the State Subject in service.[72]

3. State Subject

The number of schools and two colleges established in Jammu and Kashmir turned out a large number of matriculates and graduates every year. The minds of these young men were filled with the ideas of western political thought, freedom and equality. They demanded that only the people of Jammu and Kashmir be employed into the administration of the state and government jobs be given to them only and not to the Punjabis (people those who came from Punjab).[73]

The people of the state opposed the wholesale

usurpation of all important government posts, trade contracts, etc. in the state by the outsiders, mostly the people of the Punjab and British India.[74]

The Dogra Sadar Sabha was the first in Jammu region who paid its attention towards the protection of the rights of state subject in services and grant of scholarship to them for higher studies.

It was generally believed that it was in 1927 that for the first time, a law to protect the rights of the state subjects came into being. Actually the process started earlier. The demand was started year after year in the presidential address of Lala Hans Raj and Budh Singh. Budh Singh, a revenue officer was, known as Tyag Murti and the Father of the State, was against that many outsiders employed in government jobs in the state. Pt. Shankar Lal Koul (Publicity officer of the state) was one of the supporter of the Sabha.[75]

In 1897, Maharaja Pratap Singh had himself complained to the Government of India that his subjects were being denied their entry into state govternment services, which were almost managed by the outsiders. In May 1904, the state council adopted the rules that all deserving state subjects who sought employment in the state should be given preference in the state over others who were either outsiders or had no special qualification for appointment in the services of the state.[76] It was also provided that a candidate appointed to a post must pass through a certain period of apprenticeship in that position.[77] The Dogra Sabha as a representative body from Jammu said that all orders and rules so far issued, had not given any help to the state subjects.[78] (For the first time the term 'state subject' was defined by Maharaja Pratap Singh in June 1912, *vide* order No. 413. All *bona fide* subjects of the Maharaja were declared state subjects. Also those persons who had executed royal names and had acquired immovable property within the state territory or had continuously resided in the state for not less than 20 years were declared state subjects and also considered as eligible for state services. But these measures did not satisfied the aspirations of the people of Jammu or state and bred strong feeling of dissatisfaction among the people of the state.[79] The agitation for the state subject was spearheaded mainly by the Hindus of Kashmir and Jammu.

In 1922, at the instance of Maharaja Hari Singh, who was then the senior member of the council, a committee was appointed to define the term 'hereditary state subject' and examine the entire question of naturalisation but nothing came out of it. The committee's submission was that the object of defining the term 'state subject' was that protection be afforded and preference be given to genuine state subjects who were educationally and economically backward. [80]

The Dogra Sabha, the representative body of all sections of people in Jammu region, which had always taken a leading part in the matter of protection of their rights, tried to place true facts before the public with a view to clear the all misunderstandings.[81]

They defined in their pamphlet, *"A plea for state subject definition and genesis"* that the direct outcome of the short sighted selfish policy of the outsiders, who by taking unfair advantage of their position in the administration of the state brought the things to such a point that necessity was felt for a protective measure.[82]

Under Maharaja Hari Singh, a committee was formed on the direction of the senior and foreign members of the council. This committee consisting of six officials, non-official and representatives of the previous Jammu and Kashmir state subject committee. The commissioner represented all sections of the people, Dogra, Kashmiri and Punjabis and it was presided over by Major-General Janak Singh, the then Revenue Minister.[83]

The committee submitted its report in Jannary 1927, defining the term *'state subject'.* The rights of the state subject in services finally secured, and purchase of immovable property by non-state subjects was banned. This law with minor amendments is in force even to this day.[84]

4. Press

The press is an important medium to mould the public opinion and major thoughts and grievances of the people. Jammu region, situated in close proximity of Punjab, was always influenced by the socio-economic and political currents from Punjab. It was because of this that the Punjab press and newspaper infused a new blood, a new spirit and the new life in the minds of the people of Jammu region.[85]

In Jammu region awakening was germinated by the intelligentsia or the educated elite, which was largely brought up under the influence of the western culture on its train.[86]

In Jammu region, the press played a seminal role. The significance of the press given by and large and political leaders and people engaged in socio-cultural activities, utilised journals and daily newspapers for the purpose of disseminating their ideas and ideologies. They were radical in respect of social awakening and were convinced that without social reforms the political emancipation could not be achieved. Thus, the Jammu press assumed an important place in the life of the nation and nationalist as well as social reformers utilised it as a powerful and effective weapon against the outdated and unhealthy social customs, conventions and the unpopular policies of the government. Thus, press crystallised their urge and placed it in the open.[87]

The freedom of press in Jammu and Kashmir state is a recent growth. Before 1924, there was not a single newspaper printed or published.[88] Only *Jammu and*

Kashmir Government Gazette was the official weekly with a circulation of 900.[89] During twentieth century, a great awakening and momentous change were taking place all over the world and people of the Jammu and Kashmir state could not remain unaffected by them.[90]

The newspapers which limited number of people read came from the neighbouring province of the Punjab. *The civil and Military Gazette, the Tribunal of Lahore* and a various number of Urdu weekly magazines were circulated in the state. Whenever any person of Jammu and Kashmir state intended to write, he had to approach these newspapers. [91] The papers which were published from the Punjab and Lahore aroused the communal feelings among the Hindus and Muslims of Jammu and Kashmir state. It greatly affected the educated community of the state.[92] The important among the communal newspapers were *Akhbar-i-Am,* Lahore; *Singh Sahai,* Amritsar; *Punjab-Samachar,* Lahore, *Aina-i-kaisar of* Jallender; *Rafiq-i-Hind* of Lahore; *Punjab Gazette* of Rawal, Pindi; *Tribune, Milap* and *Pratap, etc.*[93]

In 1905, Lala Hans Raj started his first blackly newspaper known as *Dogra Gazette.* In 1906, Lala Hans Raj started another weekly paper known as *Mahajan Nite.*[94] In 1909, His Highness banned the newspaper because of their discussion on religious, political and cultural matters.[95] In 1910, again a ban was imposed all the newspapers containing raditious ideas and any one found reading or in possession of the disallowed newspapers and pamphlets was punished. [96] Ban was placed on the newspapers were *Riyasat, Siyasat* and *Inqulab,* because these newspapers attacked the administration of Dogras and criticised them.[97]

The first newspaper published in 24th June, 1924 in Jammu was the Ranbir by Mulk-Raj Saraf. The first newspaper after Press Act of 1932 was *Paswan* by Munshi Miraj-ud-Din Ahmad from Jammu on 1st July, 1932.[98]

After *Ranbir*, a number of newspapers were published which expressed the feelings of Jammu region, i.e., social, political and economic. These newspapers were *Chand* an Urdu weekly, edited by Sri Narsingh Dass Nargi,[99] *Rattan* magazine by Om Saraf; *Pukara,* Hindi weekly by Balraj puri; *Amar* of Shiv Ram Gupta; *Dogra Gazette* by Daya Krishan Girdesh; *Wattan* by Mohainder Singh, *Sudershan* by Vishwanath Kemi; *Desh Sewak* by Gopal Dutt Mengi; *Lok Sandesh* of R.S. Mukht; *Sher-e-Duggar* by D.C. Dewan; *Such* by Raja Mohd; *Akhbar* Khan from Mirpur (Now in POK), *Prabhat* and Dayanand Kapur, Shanta Bharti's Usha of *Shakuntala* and *Deepak* of Bhagnal Sharma in press 1947 period. Besides these, *Mashir Insaf* and *Kashmir Sansar* by Balraj Puri was also published.[100]

Among English newspapers or weeklies mention may be made of the *Kashmir Times* in 1934. *Kashmir Times* fought against illiteracy and advocated the establishment of a network of primary schools throughout state. Reformist and liberal minded Hindus generally found this newspaper a valuable because of its strong support in favour of social reforms; it also agitated for the protection of the rights of the state subjects. It was critical of the government policy of giving high post to non-state subjects.[101]

All social and political awakening could be attributed to a great extent to the spread of new ideas of the press. All newspapers infused new blood, new spirit, new life in the mind of the people of Jammu region. These papers voiced the grievances of the people and gave expression of their social, economic and political demands. They made people aware of the happenings in Jammu and Kashmir state.[102]

From the above, it would be clear that the press in Jammu region made a big advance from 1924-1947. To a great extent, the press did echo the social and political awakening in Jammu region and became powerful medium for creating socio-political consciousness.

5. External Influence

External influence played an important role for making Jammu people conscious for their rights. The First World War in 1914 and the Russian Revolution in 1917 left a great impact on the minds of educated youth and soldiers. In Jammu region, the soldiers who went abroad in the first world war came back with new ideas in their minds for their rights and privileges; in 1917, they watched with keen interest the destruction of Czar, the King of Russia, and the growth of new power of the people to live freely and happily without being exploited and victimised by the rich.[104]

Similarly, the Khilafat Movement led by Gandhiji in India in 1920 had a deep impact on the people of Jammu and Kashmir state, especially in Jammu region which was situated in a close proximity to Punjab. The movement evoked an enthusiasm among the people of Jammu region. For Hindus, it was a part of struggle against the British and for the Muslims it was a religious appeal.[105] On 17th March, 1920 some notices printed in the vernacular with the heading *"Jid-O-Jahad-Ke-Akheri-Faisla-Ki-Ghari"* was found pasted in Jammu.[106]

After the Khilafat Movement, the Non-cooperation movement was started by Gandhiji in 1921. This movement spread its activities in Jammu, because of the massacre at Jalianwala Bagh and Martial law administration in Punjab caused a rein of terror everywhere.[107] The bad administration in Punjab created anti-British feeling among the people of Jammu region.

Obviously, the people of Jammu joined the non-cooperation movement. Jammu students of the Prince of Wales College boycotted their classes, marched in procession raising slogans against the British authorities. They also appealed the people to remain united and face all the problems.

After boycotting the classes, they got to know that on 16th March, 1921, Gandhiji was coming to Sialkot. On hearing this news, hundreds of people from Jammu went to Sialkot to attend the meeting of the Indian National Congress. On their return, they were not only influenced with the Gandhian philosophy but also each participant was wearing a Gandhian cap. This was the beginning of the process that Indian National Congress started making or strengthening its roots in Jammu region.

The students of Prince of Wales College received a notice issued by Lala Lajpat Rai that the students of colleges affiliated to Punjab University attend a meeting at Gujranwalla on 31st March, 1921.[108] This notice was affixed on the notice board of Prince of Wales College at Jammu.[109] Despite warning given by the Principal, about 262 student, attended the meeting at Gujranwala.[110] The moving spirit behind these students was Prof Daulat Ram and two students, namely, Baldev Singh and Ishwar Das.[111] At the time of leaving for Gujranwala, they raised the slogans,[112] *"Mahatma Gandhi Ki Jai, Lala Lajpat Rai Ki Jai, Roban Son Ki-Hai, College Ki Hai".* The college authorities reacting on their act not only dismissed a number of students but closed the college. The students in protest of the government order, organised protest and demonstrations, raised the slogens-*"Mahatma Gandhi Ki Jai".* The people of Jammu also joined hands with the students, which made the situation uncontrollable and challenged the authorities in Jammu region.[113] Similarly, during the civil disobedience movement, the people of Jammu region observed complete *hartal.*[114] and students of college came out from their classes. Even including ladies took out processions in the local streets and shouted national slogans,[115] *"Mahatma Gandhi Ki Jai, Vande Matram".*

From 1904-1931, a number of social organisations emerged. These organisations were the community-based organisation working for the social, economic and political upliftment of their communities. These organisations wanted to eradicate social evils, development of education and economic upliftment of their communities. These organisations wanted to make their community politically conscious of their rights and privileges.

Cantre References

1. Sharma, S.P., *The Press : Socio-Political Awakening in Punjab and D.P.*, New Delhi, 1996, p. 50.
2. S.C., Shama, *Dogra Rule and Integration of Kashmir (1846-1949)*, 1-49.
3. Govt., J & K, Political General Department. *File No. 13/ 14 of 1904*, p. 2.
4. Singh, Narinder, *Political Awakening in Kashmir*, 1922, p. 52 and Saraf, Mulk Raj, *My Fifty Years of Journalism*, 1912, p. 78.
5. Govt. J & K Old English records, *File No. 243, of 1912*, p. 38.
6. Bashan, Vidhya, *Evolution of Democracy in Indian Policy*, New Delhi, 1989, pp. 124-125.
7. Bamzai, P.N.K., *Cultural and Political History of Kashmir*, Vol.3, 1979, p. 726.
8. Bushan, Inder, *The Govt. and Administration in Jammu and Kashmir*, Dissertation (Unpublished) Lucknow University 1942, p. 140.
9. Govt. J & K, G.P.D, *File No. 209/50 – Dof1920*, p. 15.
10. Kour, Ravinder, *Political Awakening in Kashmir*, p. 53.
11. Khan, GR, *Freedom Struggle in Kashmir*, p. 49.
12. Kour, Ravinder, *Political Awakening in Kashmir*, p. 53.
13. Govt. J & K, OER, *File No. 242/38 of 1912*, p.p 7-8 and *Census 1911*, p. 25, K Part-I, *Govt. File No. 02/ MISt 1921*, p. 5 .
14. Sharma, S.C., *"Socio-Religious Activities of the Arya Samaj in Jammu and Kashmir State." Maharshi Dayanand University Research Journal (Arts)*, Vol. 3, Number 2, Oct. 1988, p. 43.
15. *Ibid.*
16. *Ibid.*
17. *Ibid.*
18. *Ibid.*

19. *Ibid.*
20. *Census 1921*, K Part-1, p.62 and Govt. J & K, Pol. Deptt, *File No. 215 of 1917*, p. 43.
21. *File No. 157/11 of1921* D.D.G records (O.E.R.), p. 16.
22. *File No. 589/CH*, Demi-Official (Confidential) dated 8 April and *Demi Official letter from Governor of Jammu to the Home Minister to His Highness vide 526*, p. 18, April 1911 and Govt. *File No. 180 of 1921*, p. 11.
23. Sharma, S.C., *Development of Education and Community Consciousness Among the Sikhs in J &K Under Dogra Rule.*
24. *Ibid.*
25. *Ibid.*
26. Sharma, S.C., *Education and Community Consciousness Among Sikh in J&K under Dogra rule.* p. 81.
27. Sharma, S.C., *Punjab the Crucial Decade*, New Delhi, 1987. p. 140
28. Sharma, S.C., *Development of Educational Community Consciousness Among Sikhs in J & K under Dogra Rule*, p.79.
29. *Ibid.* pp. 179-89, also see S.C. Shama, Punjab the Crucial Decade. p.142.
30. Sharma, S.C., Education and Community Consciousness Among Sikh in J&K under Dogra rule, p. 81.
31. *Ibid.*
32. *Ibid.*
33. *Ibid.* p. 83.
34. *Ibid.* p. 83.
35. *Ibid.*
36. Govt. J & K General Deptt. File No. 312/7-C of 1929, List of Sabha and Societies.

37. Govt. J & K P.D., Proceeding of a meetings of Jammu and Kashmir state council held on 1 Sept. 1926, File *No. /22/F-116 of 1913.*
38. Govt. J&K P.D. File No. 267,p. 579 of 1923.
39. *Govt. J&K Pol. Dept. File No. 22/F-116 of 1913,* p. 5, List of Sabha and Societies.
40. *Govt. J&K G.D.R., File No. 162/ of 1922,* pp. 6-8. G. *J & K G.D.R., File No. 386,* p. 33 of 1923. p.7. *Maharajas order No. 396-M,* dated 25th June 1923.
41. Khan, G.H., p. 76.
42. Govt. J & K, O.E.R. F.No. 49/p. 33 of 1911, *File No. 58/ p. 34 of 1918.*
43. *Cenesus 1921,* K. Part Is p. 64., *Census 1931,* J & K Part I, p 298 and *File No. 162 of 1912, J&K File No.386/*P-33 of 1923.
44. *Cesus 1931,* J&K, Part I, p.298.
45. Govt. J & K, O.E.R., *F.No. 312/7-C of 1919* P.5. Govt. J&K, O.E.R., *F.No. 162/ of 1922* p-6.
46. Govt. J & K *File No.22/1 Year 1907,* P.12 and Sharma, B.P., Article in *Kashimir Times,* Sunday, "The Role of Dogra Sadhar Sabha", 15th Oct., 1989, P.J.
47. Govt. J&K, O.E.R., File No. 312/7-Cof 1919, pp.-5 and Govt. GE.R, *File no. 16/21 of 9,* p.7.
48. *The Dogra Gazette,* Weekly, (Urdu) Jammu, 5,1935, P.2 and Ganga Ram Wazir, President, Dogra Sabha, Dogra on Ki-Haqiqat, Tarzaman dogra Sabha (Urdu) 1959, p.2.
49. Govt. J & K General records, Pol. Deptt. *File. No. 51/1-71 of 1906,* p.12 and Sharma, B.P, Article, P.5, 1989.
50. *Ibid.*
51. *Resolution* passed by the Dogra Sadar Sabha in *Dogra Gazettee,* Dec. 5, 1935, P.2 and Govt. General records, pol. Deptt., *File No. 229,* Year 1020, p.5.

52. Order of Maharaja Hari Singh, Dated 3rd May, 1930, *A.O.R. File No. 326 of 1930, A.O.R., File No. 326 of 1930*, p.6 and *Crown file No. 291*, p.8.
53. *Ibid*-40, *Ibid.*
54. *Ibid.*
55. Govt. J & K, General records, Pol. Deptt., *File No. 327*, Year 131, P.J.
56. *The Dogra Gazette*, weekly (Urdu), Jammu, 5 Dec.1935, p.2.
57. Saraf, Mulk Raj, *J & K Encyclopedia of 1846-1946*, p.2.
58. Ganga Ram Wazir, *report*, op. cit., p.6 to 11.
59. *Ibid.* pp. 12-13.
60. General reords, P.D., also Govt. J & K Gen. PM Deptt. *File No. 711N/ 113/2-C Year 1907, p-9.*
61. Khan, G.H., p. 76.
62. Saraf, Mohammad Yousaf, op.cit., p. 525.
63. Khan, G.H., p. 76.
64. *Ibid.*
65. Singh, Nirmal, op.cit. p. 124.
66. Biscoe. C.E. Tyndate., *Fifty Years Against the Stream*, 1930, London, pp. 1-2 and *Adm. Report of Edu. Deptt. J & K 1966 (1909-10)*, p.2.
67. *A Review of Education in India*, first year book of education, Govt. of India, *National Council of Education Research*, p. 5, *Census 1931*, J & K, Part - I, p. 269.
68. *Census 1931*, J & K, Part I, p. 269.
69. *Ibid.*
70. Govt. of J & K, C.P.D. *File No. 259/5-32 of 1930*, p. 5 and *File No. 261 5 of 1931*, p. 9.
71. Govt. J&K O.E.R. File No. 40-5 of 1904, p. 5.
72. *Resolution* passed by Dogra Sadar Sabha on (18 Chet Bikram 1980 and Govt. J & K CPR *File No. 93/63-C of*

1924, pp. 5-23 and Govt. J & K G.E.R., *File No. 264/23 C of 1917*, p. 5.

73. Govt. J & K O.E.R. *File No. 40-S-18 of 1904*, p. 5.
74. National Achieves of India, *Foreign Deptt. Secret. E.* Feb. 1898 and E July 1987, p. 43.
75. *Resolution* passed by Dogra Sadar Sabha on (18 Chet Bikrarn 1980 and Govt. J & K GPR *File No. 93/63-G of 1924*, pp. 5-23 and Govl J&K C.E.R., *File No. 264/23 C of 1917*, p. 5.
76. Govt. J&K O.E.R. *File No. 40-S-18 of 1904.*, p. 7.
77. Govt. J&K O.E.R. *File No. 162 of 1904.*, p. 9.
78. *Dogra Gazetteers*, Sept. 26th, 1935, p. 7 and Oct. 3rd, 1935, pp. 10-17.
79. Govt. J & K G.P.D., *File No. 63/F-101 of 1910*, p. 5., *File No. 2 Year 1910.*
80. *A Plea for State Subject Definition and its Genesis* by Dogra Sada Sabha, Jammu, File No. 73/97-C, Year 1921.
81. *Resolution* passed by Dogra Sadar Sabha, Annual Sessions, 1919-1920.
82. *A Plea for State Subject Definition and its Genesis* by Dogra Sadar Sabha Jammu.
83. *Ibid.* File No. 63/F-I01 Year 1910.
84. *Ibid.*
85. Govt. J & K Gen., PM Deptt. *File No. 27/43-C Year* 1917-1965,p. 5 and p.5. Also Ablu Nalea, M.M., *Freedom struggle in India, 1958-1909* Delhi.
86. Ahlu Naba, M.M., *Freedom struggle In India, 1958-1909* (Delhi, 1965, p. 5.
87. *Ibid.*
88. Govt. J & K, General, Pol. Deptt., *File No. 27/43-C year 1917, File No. 131 of 1905.*
89. *File No. 150/Part II year 1910.* p. 3. Khan, Mohammed Ishaq, *History of Srinagar, 1846-1947*, Amir Publications, Srinagar, p. 195.

90. Govt. J&K, General, Pot. Deptt, *File No. 27/43-C year 1917, File No. 25/45-C year 1905.*
91. Khan, Mohammad Ishaq, *History of Srinagar*, Amir Publications, Srinagar, p. 176.
92. Singh, N.K., *Inter Communal relations in Jammu and Kashmir*, J.K. Book House. Jammu, p. 84 and *File No. 131 of 1905.*
93. Khan, G.H., *Freedom Movement in Kashmir, 1931-1940*, New Delhi, 1980, *File No. 418/P.S 149-1931.*
94. Govt. J & K, Gen., Pol Deptt. *File No. 418/PS/49/ of 1913. File No. 145-Part I year 1906.*
95. Govt. J & K, Gen., Pol, Deptt. *File No. 27/43-C, 1917. File No. 145-Part I year 1906.*
96. *Ibid.*
97. Govt. J & K, Gen., Pol. Deptt. *File No. 39/3 of 1919. File No. 10/327 year 1919.*
98. Saraf, M.R., *Fifty Years in Journalism*, p. 24, 1979 and *File No. 205/ 14-44 of1906*, p. 7.
99. Yassin, Mohammad, *Freedom struggle in Kashmir*, p. 184.
100. Kapoor, M.L., *Maharaja Hari Singh 1895-1961*, p. 109, 1989. *File No. J-31 year 1910.*
101. Khan Mohammad Ishaq, *History of Srinagar*, 1846-1947, Srinagar. p. 186.
102. Sharma, S.P., *The Press-Socio-Political Awakening*, New Delhi, 1996, P. 5.
103. Govt. J&K Gen. Pol. Dept. File No. 39/3 of 1919. File *No. 10/327 year 1919.*
104. Prog. S. No. 57-59 of 1917, Frog Pol. Deptt. Int. IB, N.A.I, p. 21.
105. Govt. J & K, Gen. Pol. Deptt. *File No. 23/31-C of 1919*, p. 21 and Govt. J & K, Gen., Pol. Deptt. *File No. 99/ C-I, March 14,1920*, p. 11 and *File No. 2000-1920*, p. 11.

106. Maula Baksh to Chief Minister, *Jammu & Kashmir state File No. 1 05/C-I,* 18 March, 1920, p. 17.
107. Bannennan to Pol. Deptt., Secy. to Govt. of India in foreign and Pol. Deptt., May 1919, National Archives of India, *Home Deptt. proceeding,* Pol., July 1919, No. 48, p. 52.
108. Bannennan to Holland, 16 May 1919, National Archive of India, *Home Deptt. Proceedings. Pol.*, July 1919, File No. 48, p. 32.
109. Daljit Singh, Chief Minister to Maula Bakash, Home Minister, J&K State. 29th Jan, 1921, J&K Pol. Deptt. *File No. 254/2 of 1921*, pp. 1-14.
110. Bannereman to Jhonwood, 17th Feb, 1921, National Archives of India, *Home Deptt. Proceedings,* Pol., Deptt. June 1921/ No. 12 and Govt. J&K Gen. Pol. Deptt. File No. 63/62 of 1921, p. 23.
111. Govt. J & K Gen. Pol. Deptt., *File No. 63/60-C of 1921.* Poll.
112. Govt. J & K, Gen., Pol. Deptt., *File No. 254/C of 1921,* p. 4 and Govt, J & K, Gen., Pol. Deptt. *File No. 63/ 60-C of 1921*, p. 10.
113. Govt. J & K, Gen., Pol. Deptt. *File No. 63/60 - cof 1921*, p. 19.
114. Bamzai, P.N.K., *"Cultural and Political History of Kashmir"*, Vol. 3, *Modern Kashmir*, p. 727.
115. Kour Ravinderjeet, p. 121.

2

JAMMU RESPONSE TO DEVELOMENT IN KASHMIR 1931-1939

The year 1931 remained a disturbing year because Hindu-Muslim riots occurred on a large scale through out the state. During the first quarter of twentieth century Maharaja Hari Singh's rule from 1925-1930 passed peacefully and was free from any communal disturbance but the situation changed in 1931, when the Hindu - Muslim riots occurred first time in Jammu region[1] i.e., reading of *Khutba*, Clash on water tank and Tohina Quran.

Reading of Khutba

On 29th April, 1931, when the Muslim were busy in the prayer, a sub-inspector of police, Babu Khem Chand, tried to stop the imam Moulvi Atta-ullah Bukhari from reading out the khutba in which the imam spoke of "Pharoah as cruel and Tyrant King". The sub-inspector warned the imam that he should stop delivering a political speech. He told the imam that only a *namaz* was permitted. The Moulvi said that he was reading the *khutba* which was as important as the *namaz* itself[2].

A protest meeting was convened on the same day at 5 PM at Talab Khatikan to condemn the behaviour of sub-inspector by Young-men Muslim Association of Jammu (An-organisation). The matter was taken to the Inspector General of Police who immediately suspended the sub-inspector.[3] Several resolutions were passed by Young-men Muslim Association to punish the polic officer for his mistake.[4]

Clash on Water Tank

On 29th April, 1931, another incident occurred at Dogore in Sambha near Jammu. Here the clash took place on the water tank which was used by both the Hindus and Muslims. Hindus claimed that tank belonged exclusively to them. On the Eid day, few Muslim used the water from the tank for their ablutions. The Muslims were provoked and complained that they had been held up and the *Eid-Namaj* delayed. They passed a resolution in which they requested Maharaja to take proper action.[5]

Tauhin-i-Quran

On 5th June, 1931, a Muslim constable, Fazaldad was found sitting on his bedding, reading *Quran*. But according to the standing orders, all beddings should be rolled up. The head constable, Labaram, remonstrated with him and rolled up his beddings and threw it on his box.[6]

Then a copy of *Panj-sura* fell upon the ground accidentally. Immediately after the incident, the constable wrote two petitions to his superior officers and third to the Young-men Muslim Association of Jammu.[7]

A public meeting was held and the Maharaja was informed about the insult of *Quran-i-Sharif*. An enquiry was made and was found that it was an accident not by deliberation.[8] The head constable was retired from his service and Muslim constable was dismissed. But the Muslims were not satisfied with this judgment and protested against the government.[9]

On 13th July, 1931, a jail incident occurred at Srinagar and created tense situation in Jammu among the Muslims.[10] Muslims of Jammu started taking out processions almost everyday and uttered slogans.

They shouted, *"Hari Singh Murdabad, Raj Kumar Murdabad, Dogra Raj Murdabad"*.

A crowd of Muslims started looting the Hindu's shops and made seditious speeches against the Dogra Raj. Young Muslim boys shouted, *"we shall shed the Hindu blood on the streets of Jammu and we shall fix the flag of Ahrar"*.[12]

On the advice of the Government of India, Maharaja immediately instituted a committee of enquiry consisting of Sir Bayor Daleal, chief justice and two other High Court Judges.[13] The Muslims and Hindus of Jammu and Srinagar boycotted the Daleal commission Report and protested against it. They took out protests the Daleal Commission Report throughout the streets and started shouting, *"Daleal Commission Murdabad"*.[14]

The government of India was at that time anxious to prevent the agitation from becoming more fierce among the Kashmiri Muslims. [15] This led to the Government of India to decide to appoint British officers to deal with the grievances of the people of the state, especially Muslims.[16]

The Government of India made a number of suggestions to the Maharaja. These were:

1. To dispatch British troops to Jammu and Mirpur and to restore peace, law and order in the disputed areas.[17]
2. To dissolve the committee of enquiry presided over by the BaynDaleal and appointment F.B.R. Spencer, retired session judge of Punjab to enquire into the causes of disturbances.
3. To enquire into the cases or any person suffering from destitution in consequences of recent

disturbances or in need of urgent relief owing to physical disablement. In disturbances or death of relatives so that the suffers would be provided for as soon as possible.

4. To provide complete religious liberty to all the state subjects. [18]
5. The Government of India also suggested to the Maharaja to accept the services of a British officer so that the Muslim agitation in the British India against the state was discredited.

At first, the Maharaja was not ready to accept this suggestion because Maharaja thought the appointment of an officer by the Government of India, whatever his nationality may, will under mine my rule and render it impossible. [19] But Maharaja's resistance could not however, stand in force of the British pressure in view of the tension which continued to increase in Punjab and in the state territory due to the Ahrar volunteers. The Maharaja accepted the appointment of the commission of enquiry. [20]

Glancy Commission

On 12th November, 1931, the Maharaja announced the appointment of commission to look into the grievances and complaints of the different communities in the state. Bertrand J. Glancy a British officer, who had served in the state in different capacities, was appointed chairman of the commission.[21] On the same day, Maharaja ordered the institute of a constitutional reforms conference to examine the feasibility of political reforms in the state. B.J. Glancy was appointed President of the conference as well. [22]

The enquiry commission headed by the B.J. Glancy was constituted of four non-official members. Two members represented the Muslims of the two provinces of Kashmir and two from Hindus of Jammu and Kashmir to enquire into the religious and secular grievances of different communities.[23] Four members were R.B. Sardar Thakur, Kartar SinghJi, K.B. Sheikh and Abdul Qayum.

Boycott of the Glancy Commission

The Glancy Commission was boycotted by both the Hindus and Muslims in Jammu region.[24] Hindus boycotted the Glancy Commission because:

1. Muslim representatives shortly after the commission started its deliberation, insisted that the Hindu law of inheritance be taken up by the commission. But Hindus opposed it because the Hindu law has an important place in *Dharm Shastras* according to which nobody was authorised to interfere with it.
2. That no question regarding cow slaughter should be raised before the commission.[25]

Muslims boycotted the Glancy Commission only to release their political prisoners. They requested the Zamindars not to pay taxes until their leader did not come back.[26]

Riots in Jammu, Mirpur, Bimber, Kotli, Reasi and Rajouri

After the Glancy Commission, political riots occurred in different areas of Jammu region. In November 1931, a agitation was led by Young-men's Muslim Association, Jammu assisted by the Ahrar invasion, to indulge in communal riots and loot Jammu city.[27]

On 25 Dec. 1931, Gauhar Rehman visited Mirpur, where he told his followers "to desist from paying land revenue to the Government" until their demands were met. This led a large number of peasants to launch a civil disobedience movement against the corrupt administration.[28]

This movement created a very tense situation in the entire tehsil and the adjacent areas. The fire of communalism was spread to different areas as Sukh-Chainpur, Seri, Kotli, Bimber, Rajouri, Kathua and Reasi, etc.[29] Many Hindus and Sikhs suffered loss of life and property. The situation became so grave that the state government was compelled to seek the services of the British Military to save the situation.[30]

On the 3rd, 5th and 7th January, 1932, violence broke out in Kotli, Kenjira Kothisolan, Samora, Khour and people were arrested at Chowmukh and Phatha Sher. On the same day, a moulvi from Kashmir reached the Rajouri Illaqa and his preaching at Dhral on that day led to the looting of some Hindu shops. On 17th January, again Darhal bazaar was looted.

There was another attack on Rajouri between 20 to 22 Jan, 1932, where the Hindus in the area between Seri were attacked and later it spread towards the Kotli and Nowshera and lastely to Bimber.[31]

On 22nd January, 1932, the Muslims of Mirpur celebrated the Mirpur Day and on the same day, the violence crupted in Kotli tehsil. Kotli Solan was burnt and mob went on to the Hindu village of Bal-Brahman and then to the village of Khui-Ratta which was also burnt at night. On the following day, Dhanna Kartot, Chowki Mong of Dana, Jangpur, Sansa and Rajua were burnt.[32] On 26 January, 1932, houses were burnt[32] in Goi, Kotli, Panjira, Serimigwar Kour, Bandali and Barmoch. The total damage in Kotli Police station was near about ten lakhs, in Seri eighteen lakhes and in Nowshera one lakes. In Nowshera, 34 Hindus accepted Islam to save their lives. In Kotli, 24 Hindus forceably accepted Islam to save their property and in Seri 435 persons accepted Islam. In Kotli, many Hindus lost their lives and one Hindu in Seri was killed. It was said 23 persons were missing in Seri.[33]

On 2nd February, 1932, Mohammandans slaughtered a cow at Baimla Tehsil Bimber and asked the one hundred Hindus to eat beef.[34] The result was that a number of Hindus, Sikhs of that area came as refugees to Jammu. They had taken shelter under the Hindu Yuvak Sabha at Jammu.[35] Some 80 families of Hindus and Sikhs of Mirpur migrated to Rawalpindi where Jammu State Hindu Relief Committee provided them relief.[36]

On 5th Feburary, 1932, a memorandum was passed by the Prime Minister in which he stated that the area was safe and all the Hindus and Sikhs, who had left their houses should go back as soon as possible and those whose houses had been burnt should delay their return for few weeks until houses have been reconstructed.[37]

Reaction in Jammu on the Bimber, Rajouri, Mirpur and Kotli Riot Cases

On 23rd January, 1932, the volunteers of Hindus Defence Force started *satyagrah* under the volunteers of P.N. Bazaz, Des Raj, Piare Lal, Banarsi Das and Haveli Ram. They wanted that Pt. Lok Nath Sharma should resign from Glancy Commission. On 24th January, 1924, they shifted to Diwan Jawala Sahai Temple and once again gring on *satyagrah* there they took an oath that until and unless Pt. Lok Nath will resign from Glancy Commission they will not take any food.[38]

On 25th January, 1932, a meeting of Hindu volunteers of the Self-Defence Force was held in Dewan Jawala Sahai Temple and there they decided that Hindus are being put to loss because of the lenient policy of the government and they should manage their own affairs themselves. P.N. Bazaz met the President of Hindu Yuvak Sabha and discussed the matter with him.[39]

As a result, Pt. Lok Nath had accepted that he would take leave from the Commission for five days but did not resign from the Glancy commission because it could create Punjabi Kashmiri question. But due to the compulsion he resigned from the commission on 31st January, 1932.[40] On the resignation of Pt. Lok Nath, the Muslims also called their representatives back from the Glancy commission.[41]

On 25th January, 1932, a *hartal* was observed in Jammu against the communal riots in Mirpur, Kotli, Bimbar, Rajouri.[42] A meeting of Hindu Yuvak Sabha was held in Diwan Jawala Sahai Temple, Jammu in which they requested the Hindus of Jammu to come to their help, as the govemment had not protected them and Muslim Raj had been established in those parts. In this meeting they requested the Maharaja Bahadur to give them a separate place which is safe for them, they also requested the people of Jammu to come as volunteers and help those people who were sufferer in riots. For this, they decided to open the office at Temple Diwan Sahai. They decided that unless and until the government satisfied them that the lives and property of Hindus are safe and culprits were not punished they would not open their shops.[43]

On 26 January, 1932, the relation between the two communities became much strained. On 1st Febuary, 1932, Hindu Yuvak Sabha received a letter from the Hindus of Bimber in which they stated that all Mohammedan population had became rebels and *bodi* or *sacred thread* of hundreds of Hindus had been cut. Hindus were asked to vacate the village.[44] Similarly, Hindus of Akhnoor, sent a telegram to seek help from Hindus of Jammu.[45]

On 7th February, 1932, Hindu Yuvak Sabha received a telegram from Mirpur, in which they were informed that 150 Hindus had been forcaibly converted to Islam at Baimla Tehsil Bimber and were forced to eat meat.[46] Hindus of Self-Defence Force received a letter from Bimber and Rajouri in which President, Hindu Yuvak

Sabha, Rajouri and Bimber, said that danger had not abated yet the S.I. (Police), who is investigating the case, will not work honestly and whole-heartedly. President of Rajouri said that the Muslims of Rajouri openly declared in the mosque that they would establish Mohammendan Raj in Rajouri.[47]

After receiving their telegrams, a complete *hartal* and protest against the government were started in Jammu city.[48] On 11th February, 1932, the Hindus of Jammu were not pleased with the subject matter of the notice *"Makhlisana Appeal'* and they said that until the perpetrators of the devastations of Mirpur and Rajouri, etc. are not punished, there can be no unity between Hindus and Mohammedans. For this a bulletin was issued by the Hindus Yuvak Sabha.[49] The volunteers of the Hindu Self-defence Force had decided to carry the work as a dictator and to carry it through a council. They started work in the Diwan Jawala Sahai Temple under the name of Relief Camp.[50]

On 14th February, 1932, the Hindu Yuvak Sabha, Jammu and Hindu Maha Sabha, Jammu observed the all India Jammu and Kashmir day.[51] A meeting was held at the Diwan Jawala Sahai Temple. A large gathering of around 300 people including 40 women attended the meeting.[52] At the outset of the meeting, S. Mohindra Singh performed an Ardas, whereas Lala Shiv Nath Nanda read out a *prarthana* in which he requested the God to come to the help of the Hindu community as it was on the verge of disaster.[53] In the meeting Pt. Daulat Ram of Hindu Yuvak Sabha said that unless th,e Hindus made a sacrifice, they would not be free from their troubles.[54]

S. Mohendra Singh while addressing the gathering said that trouble alone makes one feel for the necessity of *sangthan* (gathering). He advised the audience to leave the habit of depending on the British Government and the State Government. He said that we thought that we have to protect our cow, Brahmans and *Dharma*, but at present we have to save ourselves from loot and ruin.[55] He also advocated that our religious teachers told us to have pity on everyone and not kill any living soul. The same philosophy has been preached by Gandhiji in his non-violence movement but at the same time Mahatma Gandhi said "that I would kill one who dishonoured his womenfolk". So, when our women have been dishonoured, how can we remain silent. So, it is time not only to maintain unity but organise ourselves for the protection of our honour as "Guru Teg Bahadur Ji and Guru Gobind Singh Ji protected dharma by dent, by their courage and at the point of their so words".[56] He further that hearing of lectures and speeches would not solve their problems but to give it a practical shape, as in the past whenever there was any trouble, every house used to supply one mass means, one man and one tenth of his income for the protection of *dharma*.[57]

Recommendation of Glancy Commission in March, 1932

After the resignation of Pt. Lok Nath and other members from Jammu, the commission continued its work and submitted its report in March, 1932.[58]

1. It recommended that minimum qualification for appointment to a government post should not be pitched unnecessarily high and effective measures should be taken if any community was going to be neglected.
2. It also recommended that the grant of proprietary rights in respect to all "land of which the ownership is retained by the state and the right of occupancy is enjoyed by private persons." It also recommended the abolition of several vexatious taxes and laid great emphasis on the

removal of unemployment by promoting industries in the state.[59]

3. Another step was the removal of restrictions that existed on the Freedom of Press and the platform.[60]

In reaction to the Glancy Commission report the people of Jammu region started a number of agitations. In April 1932, agitation was started by the Hindus of Mirpur against the report. S. Mohinder Singh and his fellow men were arrested and were sentenced to six months rigorous imprisonment. In this agitation all Hindus, i.e., Mahajans, Brahmans, Khatris and Sikhs joined their hands against the recommendations of the Glancy Commission. The situation was handled by the Punjab Police with Lathi charge. Twenty five Hindu leaders were arrested.[61] Hindu Maha Sabha termed the Glancy Commission report a one-sided report, which gives definite encouragement to communalism.

1. By recommending that for services in all department minimum standard of efficiency should be fixed instead of maximum available and the principle of comparative merit should be disregarded to the disadvantage of culturally advance communities like Hindus and Sikhs.[62]
2. Encouragement was given to the Muslims for literary education, and scholarship was awarded to the son's of Muslim craftsmen but no recommendation for teaching arts and crafts to Hindus.
3. The Hindu Maha Sabha warned the British Government against the evil consequences of carrying Anglo-Muslim alliances.[63]

Grievances presented to the Glancy Commission by the Hindu, Sikhs and Muslims of Jammu Region

While the commission was conducting its enquiry in state, events were moving very fast. Roused from the long political slumber, the people were clamouring for their basic rights. Each community was voicing its grilvances, which to the surprise of all were fundamentally the same.[64]

Hindu Grievances

In the year 1932, memorials and representations was submitted by the Brahman Sabha, Jammu, in which they stated.[65]

1. That the claims of Dogra Brahmins are being ignored by His Highness Government and that the members of the Dogra Brahmin community were signed out for premature retirement.
2. It was requested that appointments and scholarships may be reserved for Dogra Brahmin and practice of retiring Dogra Brahmins prematurely should be stopped.

On 12th October, 1932, the Rajput Amar Sabha submitted a memorial to His Highness Maharaja Bhadur, in which they submitted that every community in the state is aspired and is up asking for rights and concessions, it seems that the Rajputs as a community should also consider it necessary to approach Your Highness for their rights and privileges.[66]

They submitted that, Rajputs as warriors, occupied a unique position in the state. By dint of their devotion to the royal family and their contribution to state forces, they should be given first right to serve for the ruling family.[67]

Highlighting their service to the *Darbar*, they submitted that:

1. The special scholarships may be provided for Rajputs so that they may not remain backward in education and may come up along side other communities.

2. Special consideration may graciously be shown to them in the matter of the enlistment to civil services of the state.
3. Cultivable state lands may graciously be granted to them and they may be declared an agricultural tribe under the Land Alienation Regulation.[68]
4. Special seats may be reserved for the Assembly which is shortly proposed to be established in the state.
5. One post of a minister may be graciously reserved for them.
6. They may graciously be exempted from the Arms Regulation. They have to keep arms as a matter of religion.
7. Foreign scholarships may also be graciously allotted to them.[69]

On 29th March, 1932, a representation of Hindus was submitted to His Excellency viceroy in which they stated that almost all Hindu subjects of Rajouri tehsil have not been only looted by the Mohammedan rebels, but their houses have been burnt, their ladies have been molested and some of the Hindus have been enforced to become Muslims. Their sacred places have been dismantled and idols have been broken. They requested that the following necessary measures may kindly be taken so that their lives, religion and property may be safe.[70]

They demanded that:[71]

1. Strict law may kindly be applied for their punishment.
2. Rajouri town may kindly be made permanent military head-quarters.
3. The town may be connected with others by lorry roads.
4. The Muslim *lambardars, zaildars*, pensioners and *jagirdar* rebels should be punished and Bakarwals who took an active part in the rebellion may be disallowed to enter Rajouri Tehsil.

5. No Muslim (*Moulvis*) may be permitted to lecture without permission.
6. Collective fines may kindly be levied upon the Mohammadan rebels, who looted the Hindus in Rajouri and Reasi.
7. As the Land Alienation Act, Agriculturists Relief Act of 1983 and the legal prohibitation of *"Begar"* have encouraged the Muslim rebels, therefore these acts may kindly be abolished.
8. Necessary facilities and steps may be taken in resetting the looted Hindus in their respective villages and necessary arrangement may kindly be made for their safety in future.[72]

The Maharaja was warned that in future no harm should come to Hindus and their property.[73]

Sikh Grievances

A conference of Sikh representatives was held on 15th,16th and 17th May, 1932, at Mirpur and a resolution was passed which was presented before the Prime Minister, to take necessary action against the unrest prevailing among Sikhs in the state due to the non-fulfillment of the pledges and assurances given by the *Darbar* at the time of the appointment of Glancy Commission and an account of the undignified treatment accorded to them in the matter of distribution of seats on the proposed assembly. They express strong resentment at negligible representation given to them in the constitution.[74]

The Sikh expressed its strong indignation and disappointment on the fact that despite of their representation and consequent promises of the state darbar, the state government had not removed their grievances as they had done so in the case of Muslims.

These representation in the state and services was less according to their qualification. Their appointment in the police and Army was not good.

They demanded that:[75]

1. Grant-in-aid should be given to the Sikhs and girls school be open Better education for Sikh boys and girls and scholarships should be reserved for them. Some facilities should be given to them as given to Muslims by Glancy Commission.
2. One member of the state cabinet should always be a Sikh.
3. Adequate provision should be made for teaching Punjabi language and Gurmukhi script for boys and girls.
4. Management of Sikh shrines and places of worship should be handed over to the Sikhs.
5. One-Third representatives should be in the legislative assembly.
6. There should be a religious library for Sikhs.
7. Law of inheritance not to be introduced with.
8. Repeal of Land Alienation Act.
9. Abolition of the grazing taxes in the villages and reduction of grazing taxes on lands.
10. Reduction of land revenue rates and considerable remission of revenue in Jammu.
11. Grant to permission for Sikhs to keep arms.
12. Freedom of speech and press.
13. Correction of census figure.
14. Admission of Sikhs in the military training school at Jammu.
15. Definition of "State Subject" to be amended to the extent, *Rayatnama* should be sufficient for getting the status of the state-subject.

16. Levy of tax of one *anna* per rupee of land revenue on Sikh zamindars.
17. More Sikhs should be taken in the state civil services.
18. Sikh should be compose twenty five per cent of the state military and police.

On 30th May, 1932, another deputation of the Sikhs of Mirpur met the Colven member of the Clancy Commission in Jammu and mentioned certain demands:[76]

1. The existing walls of Gurdwara of Mirpur rendered unfit, hence should be constructed fresh to ensure stability and safety and should be built at state expenses.
2. Properties burnt or looted inside the Gurudawara, the religious sacred books essential to the performance and observance of religious ceremonies to be restored and supplied.
3. State Subjects whose houses have been burnt and property robbed should be given suitable places to rebuilt their houses and enable to stall business.
4. Compensation to be given to the those refugees who had taken shelter in the British territories, i.e., Rawalpindi, Jhelum, Lalamusa, Gujrat and Gujrawala, etc. Monthly allowance should be given to them so that they can maintain their families till such time that they are able to return to their villages.
5. The forceable conversions of the Sikhs to Islam have been effected in the Jammu region, especially in Mirpur and Rajouri districts. It is submitted that steps should be taken to stop the conversion.

6. Every steps should be taken to bring the law breakers to book and to punish them so that minority communities should feel secured in future.
7. State Arms Act Rules should be framed so that Sikhs and Hindus tradesmen might obtain gun licenses without any difficulty and can protect themselves and their property.
8. The managing committees of Gurdawaras in the state should be treated on the same lines as the managing committee of Mosques.
9. The state should facilitate acquisition of land at village Pindi, Sabarwal and Sikh Chainpur of Mirpur tehsil and at the village Ali Beg of Bimber tehsil, so that colonies might be established for Hindus and Sikhs shopkeepers.

Muslim Grievances

Glancy Commission had received a number of statements regarding grievances of Muslim zamindars.[77]

They demanded that:

1. Under the Islamic injunctions' a Muslim cannot use the water of a spring or a well which has been touched by an impure persons or the water which has been drawn by one who eats dead animals. It is, therefore, requested that orders should be issued that no sweeper or Dom law caste should take water without permission from such springs or wells as are all possession of Muslims.
2. The mosques which were constructed during Mughal period in tehsil Bimber and are at present in the possession of the state should be re-constructed. These are *Shashi* Masjid at Nowshara outside Serai, two mosques within the Serai and mosque at Manawar.

3. Middle schools should be started in the hilly area in Bimber.
4. Many Muslims in Mirpur were deprived of their Jagirs as are given to them by Mughal rulers. So, they should be allowed to remains same during Dogra rule and they should be not be deprived of the title of *Jagirdars.*
5. Medicines and articles for domestic use should be exempt from custom duty.
6. Regulation for compulsory education should also be extended to such villages where the numbers of school-going boys are proportionately final. The regulation may be withdrawn when the number of boys in school increases.
7. They requested that strict action should be taken against the *Tehsildar* of Akhnoor who ordered them to stop the shout of *"Allah-O-Akbar"*[78]
8. Muslim *Panches* should also be appointed in Akhnoor as there are all Hindu *Panches* and as half of the population in Akhnoor town are Muslims.
9. Muslims of Bhadrawah have brought under cultivation basin jungle from times past but with all this they have been granted only the right of "*Malguzar*" instead of proprietary rights over these lands by the settlement department.
10. There were no satisfactory arrangements for the education of Muslim girls.
11. A shop tax Rs 12 which has been imposed on the Muslim shopkeepers is unbearable.
12. There are two Hindu *Lamberdars* in Bhadarwah. Muslim want all high posts and *Lamberdar's* post should be given to the Muslims.[79]
13. Fifty per cent of Muslims representation in services.

14. Remission of the grazing tax.
15. Abolition of *Begar*.
16. No trouble for those who accepted Islam with their own will.
17. Appointment of Muslim teachers and stress on religious education for Muslim children.[80]

On 9th March, 1932, a representation was submitted to Prime Minister by the Anjuiman Islamia, Jammu.[81] In their representation they laid stress on:

1. Their representation in seventh regiment should be at least half.
2. Muslim recruiting for bodyguard, cavalry should be thrown open and the existing vacancies should be filled up with Muslim recruits.
3. The Muslim representation in civil services should be increased so that their economic and social position should be improve.[82]
4. They said no representation of Anjumian Islamia had been invited to the constitutional conference, to be held on 14th March, 1932, under Mr Glancy. It is prayed that Muslim representation may kindly be increased and representation of Anjuman should be invited.[83]

Glancy submitted its report to Maharaja in May 1932, in which he recommended that Legislative Assembly be established as soon as possible and made suggestion regarding its composition, power and functions. According to him, its tenure should be three years and it could meet twice a year. Assembly should have an elected majority. The assembly was vested with the powers to legislate on all subjects, except those reserved for the exclusive control of Maharaja, namely, foreign relations and state forces. He recommended it could seem a fair solution that the total member should be equal to two-thirds of the member of the elected members.[84]

Glancy recommended the limitation be imposed on the introduction of private bills in the assembly and no taxes should be imposed and no monopolies should be granted by the government without making a reference to the Sabha.[85]

Glancy recommended separate electorate and joint electorate, a dangerous experiment and distrust between the different communities. His Highness in Council was pleased to accept the recommendation of the Glancy Commission. An opportunity was given to all the members of the community to express their opinion.[86] From Jammu region, Col Sansar Singh said, "It was right time for such a change in the state".[87]

According to Lala Thakur Dass, "It is pre-mature to introduce an elected assembly. He said it was dangerous to entrust the government with the responsibility on those who had been responsible for recent communal outbreaks in the state. He emphasised in British India, too, beginning was made through local bodies and only there it had attained present position. He said, "Jammu and Kashmir is far behind in education and general advancement, therefore, first ground be prepared for such a change".[88]

Sardar Lala Singh said the safeguards should be introduced in the proposed constitution so that minority community should not suffer by the hands of majority community.[89]

After constitutional reforms, it was suggested by B.J. Glancy to appoint the Franchise Committee to examine the franchise qualifications of the voters and to collect the necessary data on which further action could be based.[90] Franchise committee took two years to complete its work.[91]

The Franchise Committee recommended the a Legislative Assembly on the Morly-Minto model be established, with the object of identifying the people with administration. In other words, it recommended a council with non-official majority which would pass legislative assembly, ask questions, discuss budget and pass resolution.[92] The Franchise Committee rejected the direct election for frontier area of Laddakh and Gilgit, giving them three Muslim and two Buddhists seats in the assembly for Poonch and Chenani *Jagirs*, two Muslims for Franchise elections and two Hindus seats by nomination. One official nominated by *Haqadar* of Chenani was also recommended.[93]

Many changes were made by Franchise Committee in Glancy scheme of constitution. The recommendation of the Franchise Committee was criticised by all the people of Jammu and Kashmir, i.e., Both Hindus and Muslims.[94]

The Hindus complained that the report had enslaved them to the majority of Muslim members in the assembly. The Muslims criticised it for having given under-weight to arbitrary fixed constituencies and relegate numerical and other facts alone to weigh with the authors of the constitutional law, to a secondary position.[95] Lastly, Franchise Committee failed to satisfy the people's aspirations.[96]

Jammu and Kashmir Muslim Conference

On 16th October, 1932, the Jammu and Kashmir Muslim Conference was formed under the Presidentship of Sheikh Mohammad Abdullah. It was communal in nature, working for the welfare of Muslim of Kashmir. The Muslim of Jammu did not show any sympathy towards Sheikh Abdullah and his Muslim Conference in the early phase.[97]

On 7th May, 1933, a resolution was passed by the Hindu Youth Conference of Jammu, requesting the Maharaja to graciously repeal all such laws and circulars as sub divide state subject into different classes and ordered them entry into the state service, civil military, and disable them for state scholarship to prevent them from election to proposed assembly and disqualify them from acquiring immovable property within the state, because this policy of discrimination had created much disaffection and estrangement between the different classes of state subject and was likely to widen the gulf day by day.[98]

In their opinion, economic distress was the main cause of the unrest and disturbance. They wanted a proper recommendation for economic peace and prosperity. They recalled with distress the Hindu victims from riots had been given adequate protection, much less compensated for their losses, their lives and honour were still in danger.[99]

The Constitution Act, 1934: Praja Sabha

In April 1934, the Maharaja promulgated the constitution Act of 1934. The Constitution Act was based on the recommendation made by the Constitutional Reforms Conference and the Franchise Committee.[100] The Act provided for the reconstitution of the government of the state and the institution of the ;egislative assembly. The provisions were envisaged by the act for the constitution of a council of ministers appointed by the Maharaja and responsible to him. Certain powers of the government were reserved by the Maharaja for him and exclusively for his control. The powers left in the presidium were vested with the council of ministers to be exercised by it.[102]

The legislative assembly known as the Praja Sabha, was consisted of 75 members out of whom 33 were to be elected for constituencies of different communities on a franchise which did not cover more than three per cent of the population. Sixteen of the members were to be nominated for special constituencies. Besides the elected and the nominated members, the assembly had fourteen other members who were appointed by the

Maharaja and twelve official members who were appointed by the assembly by virtue of their office and among whom were included the ministers of the state. The tenure of the assembly was fixed at three years unless it was dissolved earlier, or its term was extended for special circumstances. The Maharaja also reserved the powers to summon meet in two sessions in a year, in March, at Jammu and in October in Srinagar. The Maharaja retained the right to summon the assembly for ordinary or special session at such time and places as he deemed fit.[103]

The *Praja Sabha* members could ask questions, move resolutions, introduce bills and discuss the state budget, but any bill passed by the Praja Sabha was sent back for reconsideration together with amendments.[104]

The first election of Praja Sabha was held on 3rd September, 1934. The election was a landmark in the history of Jammu and Kashmir state.[105] But the constitution and the assembly given under the regulation Act of 1991 samwat did not rise up to the expectations of the people.[106]

The elected representatives both Muslims and non-Muslims were disenchanted with constitution and they felt for the need for a fresh constitution change in the state. This feeling gave rise to the joint action for the demand of a responsible government in the state.[107]

Struggle for the Responsible Government

The struggle for the achievement of a responsible government was the crux of the freedom movement in Jammu and Kashmir state.[108] The demand for the establishment of a responsible government in Jammu and Kashmir state made for the first time by the radical Muslim young men in 1934 assumed stigmatic importance in 1935, when a protest against the dissatisfactory character of the legislative assembly was launched by the popular representatives of Kashmir.[109] They declared to observe a

Responsible government Day on 8th May, 1936, throughout the state.[110]

Sheikh Mohammad Abdullah issued an appeal to all the people of Jammu region to participate in this movement for responsible government.[111] Except for a few progressive Hindus, the non-Muslims in general did not respond to Sheikh Abdullah's call because of the fear of insecurity.[112]

According to the Hindu leaders, i.e., S. Budh Singh, Pt. Prem Nath Bazaz, the cry for responsible government was useless and the demand for its establishment was meant only to snatch the government from them.[113]

By-Election, 1937

The first by-elections to the legislative assembly took place in 1937.[114] The consequence of the by-elections convinced the non-Muslim of the genuineness of the demand for establishment of responsible government. Several non-Muslim elected to the assembly had realised that the assembly was a 'mock show' and that it needed democratisation. This realisation resulted in a greater integration between the Muslim and the non-Muslim in due course of time. Also, it brought new developments on political scene.[115]

Cow Slaughter Case

Towards the end of June, 1937, an agitation was started by Hindus over the Judgement of Jammu High Court in the case of cow slaughter.[116] Chief Justice Sheikh Abdullah Qayoon and Justice Jankinath Wazir reduced the sentence which was passed by the subordinate court from 7 years to give rigorous imprisonment of one year. It was held the offence was not committed to wound anybody's religious feeling and suspectabilities but what they had done, had been done secretly at night.[117]

The Hindus, Sikhs of Jammu started a campaign of agitation against it. [118] A number of meetings were held in temple named Dewan-Jawala Shahi in Jammu. This temple was the centre of agitation. Seventy Women also had given their participation and took a procession *in* front of the Civil hospital. The women laid themselves flat on the ground. The police started lathi-charge on the women. 35 women got injuries and six were arrested. [119]

The result of this was that, a procession of the people in Jammu region emerged. They uttered slogans, *"Aurton par-lathi charge karni wali police murda bad, Justice Qayoom, Justice Janki Dass murdabad."*[120]

A number of resolutions were passed by the working committee of Hindu Sabha. They expressed great sympathy with the satya graha in Jammu, who had suffered in a protest against the relaxation for the law in the case of cow slaughters and called upon the *Darbar* to reassure the Hindus that recent High Court judgement would not serve as a precedent in the case of cow slaughter in future. [121] On 24th August, 1937, a procession of about 200 women, 150 men took place near Dewan Jawala Shahi temple. About 200 persons were arrested along with 25 women. [122]

The result was the government issued two communiques explaining that High Court judgment did not involve any change in law regarding cow-laughter. [123] On this, on 16th August, 1937, the people of Jammu started agitation against the government. [124]

National Demand and Jammu

On 27th August,1938, while the agitation for responsible government was in progress. The leaders among whom were Sheikh Abdullah, Bakshi Gulam Mohammad, Khwaja Gulam Mohammad Sadiq, Maulana

Sayeed Masoodi, Sardar Budh Singh, Pt Kashyab Bandhu, Pt Prem Nath Bazaz and Pt. Sham Lal Saraf drafted a joint memorandum on responsible government. The memorandum was called "National Demand".[125] The ultimate goal of this National Demand was to being social and political outlook and to achieve responsible government under the aegis of the Maharaja. [126]

But this National Demand was criticised by people of Jammu because according to them, the National Demand was not based on any economic motive but it stood for the achievement of political power for Muslim supremacy. [127]

It was not accepted by the Hindus of Jammu. It was said the manifesto of National Demand was not of a truly representative character. It was not signed by the non-Muslim and Yuvak Sabha of Kashmiri Pandit. [128]

National Conference

Sheikh Abdullah, the president of the Muslim Conference, realised that without the help of non-Muslims of the state his party would not be successful. [129] At that time Sheikh Abdullah strengthened his relation with National Congress and their leader Nehru. Nehru advised the Conference leaders to convert the Muslim conference into a National Conference. [130]

On 28th June, 1938, a meeting of the working committee of the Muslim Conference was held in which Sheikh Abdullah moved a resolution suggesting to change the name of Conference to "National Conference" and to amend the constitution as to throw its *"door open"* to non-Muslims irrespective of their caste, creed or religion. So, he gave a secular turn to his policies.[131] He met various Hindu leaders, i.e., M.R. Saraf, S. Budh Singh, etc.

These developments led to the foundation of National Conference on 11th June, 1939.[132] Sheikh Abdullah visited Jammu for a number of times and spent long hours developing his contacts with prominent local people of Jammu, so that he could lay the foundation of National Conference in Jammu. [133]

Sheikh Abdullah was not popular in Jammu region when he opened the doors for the Hindus and Muslims of Jammu. The people of Jammu region refused to join the National Conference.[134] The National Conference movement could not penetrate deeply into the rural areas of Jammu region preferred the National Congress than the National Conference.[135]

Constitution Act of 1939

In 1939, the Maharaja ordered the repeal of the constitution Act of 1934 and promulgated a new constitutionald. Act for the government of the state.[136] The new Constitutional. provisions were aimed to placate the rising temper of the people in the state and their incessant demand for self-government.[137] The new constitution Act of 1939 proved *for from* satisfactory and was bitterly criticised.[138]

So, from 1931-1939, a communal feeling and agitation started in Jammu region which led to the appointment of Glancy Commission, Muslim Conference and in 1934 constituted the Praja Sabha to aid and advice the ruler. Later to mobilise the Jammu people, the Muslim Conference changed themselves to National Conference in 1939 but never became a major political force among the Hindus of Jammu region.

Ends and References

Govt J & K, Gen, Pol. Deptt., *File No. 420 of 1932*, pp. 9-14 and *File No. 327 of 1931*, p. 21.

2. Govt J & K, Gon, Pol., Deptt., *File No. 13/14 of1931*, p.14, and *File No. 10/20 of 1931*, p. 5.
3. H.H. Govt. J & K, Gen, Pol. Deptt. *File No. 485 of 1931*, p. 21, and *Note* by G. E.C. Make Field on unrest among muslims of Jammu and File No. 13/14 of1931, p. 10, and *Adm. Report of 1930-1933*, p. 2.
4. *Ibid.*
5. *Ibid, Report of the enquiry into disturbances in Jammu* in 1932, pp. 92-42.
6. *Investigation into Mohammad and tension in Jammu*, Govt. J & K Pol. Deptt., File No. 12 of 1931 p. 43 and National Archives of India, Home Deptt., Pol., File No. 18, June 1931, p. 2.
7. *Ibid.*
8. *Ibid* and *Report* of enquiry into disturbances in Jammu in 1932.
9. *Ibid.*
10. Khan, G. H., pp. 134-135.
11. J & K State Archive, Jammu, *File No. 92, year 1932*, p. 7.
12. Govt., J & K., Govt., Pol., Deptt., *File No. 93110 of 1931*, p. 2.
13. Koul, Teng and Bhat, *Constitutional History of Jammu and Kashmir 1981*, p. 80.
14. *File No. 92/-C, year 1932*, pp. 3-7 and *File NO.93110 of 1931*, P. 5 and *File No. 63/-C, year 1932*, p. 7 and *Administrative report*, 1930-31-32-33, p. 123.
15. *Telegram to the Resident in Kashmir*, No. 2509 5, Oct. 8, 1931, File No. 423, p. 2, Political Deptt., 1931 N.A.I.
16. *Letters from the Resident in Kashmir to His Highness the Maharaja of J &K*, Oct. 14, 1931, p. 4 and *Ibid*.

17. *Ordinance No. of 1931*, National Achieve of India. Home Deptt., *Political File No.13/23*, p. 7.
18. *Teligram from the Resident*, Pol. India, New Delhi - No. XX and R 122-C dated 9th Nov., 1931, National Achieve of India, Home and Pol., Deptt., 1931 p. 10.
19. *Letters from His Highness of Maharaja of Jammu & Kashmir to the resident in Kashmir*, Oct. 7, 1931 File No. 423, p. 2, Home-Pol. Deptt., 1931, N.A.I.
20. *Ibid*.
21. The *Ranbir*, weekly (Jammu), May 2nd,1931, p. 7.
22. *Ibid* and Maharaja Hari Singh's order dated 24 Nov., 1931, pp. 1-5.
23. *Glancy Commission Report*, pp. 7-10 and *Commission* appointed the under order of the Maharaja under the chairmanship of B.J. Glancy to enquire in the grievances and complaints of the people of the stale, 12th Nov., 1931.
24. The Ranbir, weekly (Jammu), 2 May, 1931, p. 7.
25. *Commission* appointed under the orders of the Maharaja under the chairmanship of B.G. Glancy to enquire in the grievances and complaints of the people of the state.12 Nov., 1931 and Govt. J & K Pol., *Gen. Records, File No. 84/29 of 1931*, p. 3, and *File No. 424 of 1931*, p. 5.
26. *Govt. J & K Pol. Gen. Records*, File No. 167/29 of 1931, p. 2 and File No. 138 of 1931, p. 2 and File No. 138 of 1931, p. 2.
27. *File No. 422 of 1932, Govt. Pol. Deptt. Jammu*, p. 27.
28. *Ibid*.
29. *Ibid.*
30. *Ibid.*
31. *Ibid.*
32. *Ibid.*
33. *Ibid.*

34. *File No. 109 of 1932*, Govt. Pol. Deptt., Jammu, p. 11.
35. *File No. 109 of 1932*, Govt. Pol. Deptt., Jammu, p. 16.
36. *Ibid.*
37. *Ibid.*, p. 21.
38. *File No. 90/39-1932* of Pol. Deptt., 1932, pp. 11-14.
39. *Ibid.*
40. *Ibid.*
41. *Ibid.*
42. *File No. 90/39 of 1932,* Govt. J&K Pol. Deptt. Jammu pp. 7-10.
43. *Ibid.*
44. *Ibid.*
45. *Ibid.*
46. *File No. CS-P. B-94 of 1932* Govt J&K Pol. Deptt., p. 5.
47. *Ibid.*
48. *File No. 90/39 of 1932* Govt. J&K Pol. Deptt., p. 10.
49. *Ibid.*
52. *Ibid.*
53. *Ibid.*
54. *Ibid.*
55. *Ibid.*
56. *Ibid.*
57. *Ibid.*
58. *Report of the Grievances Enquiry Commission of 1932*, p. 51.
59. *Ibid,* p. 32.
60. *Administrative Report*, p. 32, 1932.
61. *File No. 258, year 1932*, Govt. J &K, Pol. Deptt. Jammu, p. 12.
62. *File No. 192JPS/-169 year 1932*, Govt. Pol. Deptt. Jammu, p. 3.
63. *Ibid.*, p. 5.

64. Bamzai, P.N.K., Vol. 3, *Cultural and Political History of Kashmir*, M.D. Publication Pvt. Ltd. New Delhi, 1994, p. 735.
65. *File No. PS 208/217 year 1932*, Govt. J & K Pol. Deptt., pp. 5-7.
66. *File No. 190/92, year 1932*, Govt. J & K Pol. Deptt., p. 9.
67. *Ibid.*
68. *Ibid.*
69. *Ibid.*
70. *File No. 192/PS-169 of 1932*, pp. 2-7 and *File No. 134/ 43 PS of 1932*, pp. 1-5 and *File No. 190/292 of 1932*, pp. 4-5 and *File No. 407/PS. 153 of 1932*, pp. 2-5, Jammu.
71. *Ibid.*
72. *Ibid.*
73. *File No. 92/173 of 1932*. Govt. J & K Pol. Deptt. p. 5 and *File No. 12/ PS of 1931*, J & K Pol. Deptt., p. 3.
74. *File No. 297/88 of 1932*. Govt. J & K. Pol. Deptt., p. 3 and File No. 487 - PS 88 of 1932, Govt. J & K Pol. Deptt. pp. 1-3.
75. *Ibid*, pp. 1-7 .
76. *File No. 156/8-8-93 of 1932*. Govt. J &K. Pol. Deptt., pp. 312 and *File No. PS 200/194 of 1932*. Govt. J&K. Pol. Deptt., pp. I-7 and *File No. 487. PS of 1932*. Govt. J&K Pol. Deptt., pp. 1-7.
77. *File No. 267/PS 579 of 1932*, Govt. J & K Gen. Pol. Deptt., pp . 3-11.S.
78. *Ibid.*
79. *Ibid.*
80. *File No. 268/301/PS-1932*, Govt. J & K, Gen. Deptt., p. 5.
81. *File no. 267 IPS 79 of 1932*, Govt. J & K, Gen. Deptt., p. 9.

82. *Ibid.*
83. *Ibid.*
84. *Ibid,* op. cit., p . 4 .
85. *File No. 62 of 1932,* J & K Pol. Deptt., p. 19 and *Ibid.*
86. *File No. 232/1-PAS, Year 1932,* Govt. J & K Pol. Deptt., p. 269.
87. *Ibid.*
88. *Ibid,* p. 271 .
89. *Ibid.*
90. *Report of Franchise Committee,* p 1 .
91. *Ibid.*
92. *Ibid,* P. l, and *J & K Govt. Gazettee,* Vol. 149, dated 20 Jan., 1934 and *Census of India, 1941,* Vol. XXII State, Part -1, p. 5.
93. *The Franchise Committee Report,* p. 5.
94. *Ibid,* pp . 5-7.
95. *Ibid.*
96. *The Statesman*, Calcutta, 15 Feb. 1935, p.13.
97. Bazaz, P.N., p. 736.
98. *File No. 590/1953*, Govt J&K Pol. Deptt., p. 9.
99. *Ibid.*
100. Manbekar, D.R., *Indian Princess*, 1979, p. 33.
101. *Ibid.*
102. *The Stateman,* Calcutta, 20 April 1935, p. 9.
103. *File No. 74-P year 1934*, Foreign and Pol. Deptt. No. 1-10.
104. *J&K Regulation No. l of 1941 Samwat*, Section. 35.
105. *The Statsman* (Calcutta), 20th Sept., 1934, p. 9.
106. Bazaz, P.N., *Inside Kashmir*, Srinagar, Kashmir 1941, p. 385.
107. Khan, G.H., op. cit., p. 250.
108. *Ibid.*

109. *Ibid.*
110. *Ibid.*, p. 265.
111. *File No. 128/B - 446/38-1938,* Part - II, Govt. J &K. Pol. Deptt, p. 4.
112. *Ibid.*
113. *The Tribune* (Lahore) 7 Oct., 193b, p. 16.
114. *Hamdard*, weekly, Srinagar. 23 Jan., 1937. p. 6.
115. *Ibid.* P. 11.
116. *File No. 41/P. IS, year 1937*, Govt. J&K. Pol. Deptt. and Govt. Pol. Deptt., File no. 31/D-16 of 1937. p. 3.
117. *Ibid.* p. 4.
118. *File No. 31/6 of 1937*, p. 4 and Adm. Report J&K state. Samwat 1993-94, p. 11.
119. File No. 174/D-22 of 1937. Govt. J&K, Pol. Deptt., P. 3 and *File No. 41, P-IS, year 1937*, p. 7, Govt. J&K Pol. Deptt.
120. *File No. 44-D-15 of 1937*, Govt. J&K, Pol. Deptt., p. 9.
121. *Ibid.*
122. *Ibid.*
123. *Annual Adm. Report J & K State Samwat, 1993-94*, pp. 1-7.
124. *File No. 31/D-6, year 1937*, Govt. Pol. Deptt., p. 9.
125. *National demand*, 1938 Published by All India State's people's, Conference, Bombay, pp. 5-16.
126. *Ibid.*
127. *The Tribune* (Lahore), Sept. 1937, p. 4 and Nov. 1938 p. 5.
128. *Ibid.*
129. In federal scheme, the British want to unite Indian states with the rest of India. It was the outcome of the Govt. of Indian Act. 1935.

130. Saxena, H.L., p. 239.
131. *Ibid* and Saraf, M.R., p. 155.
132. *Ibid.*
133. Saraf, M.R. op. cit., pp 155-156.
134. Saxena, H.L., p. 239.
135. Yassien, Mohammed, p. 79
136. *Jammu and Kashmir Constitution Act of 1939*, Section 11-12, pp. 5-10.
137. *Ibid.* Sec-12. pp. 7- I 2.
138. *Ibid.* See-56. p. 23.

3

JAMMU IN WAR YEARS, 1939-1945

The World War II saw the growing importance of the Maharaja with the British Government. He gave unstinted help and support to them and placed all his resources at the disposal of the Government of India. Consequently, he was appointed to the imperial war cabinet and in this capacity he toured the allied front in the middle east. Any action that he took against the people's mreceived support from the imperial government.[1]

World War II

The peace that was ushered in after the World War had always been an uneasy one. Although, there was no war during the next twemty years. The threat had cropped up every now and then. The Germany had no doubt accepted military defeat but she had not accepted the peace that was thrust upon her. Through the Treaty of Versailles, Germany had been deprived of her colonies and quite a lot of her territory and population. Besides, the clause in the treaty was known to be most unjust and one that was aimed at breaking Germany economically. In short, the Germans considered the peace as dictated and never felt morally bound to adhere to the terms and conditions of the treaty. As a result, the Germans had been on the look out for an opportunity to cut the shackles with which she had been bound by the Treaty of Vassailles.[2] This opportunity came by way of the growing clash of interests between the major powers of Europe, each of whom planned to use Germany against the other for its own ends. This infighting among the European powers had left the League of Nations defunct and Germany could now flout the terms of the peace treaty with impunity. The rise of Nazism and the emergence of leaders of the caliber of Hitler in Germany gave her the capability of exploiting the situation for growing militarily from strength to strength.[3] Subsequently, when it was realised that Germany had grown dangerously strong, the fear of an armed conflict with her made the other military powers of Europe to follow a policy of appeasement, which, in fact, brought the prospects of a war even closer.

Twenty years of peace was finally shattered when Germany invaded Poland on 1st September, 1939. The war, so started, remained localised only for 48 hours. On Sunday, September 3, 1939 at 8.30 pm, the Viceroy Lord Linlithgow announced over the All India Radio that the Government of the Majesty "was engaged in a war with Germany". This evoked a prompt response from Hari Singh, the Maharaja of Jammu and Kashmir, who placed his personal services at the disposal of the Majesty, the British Crown.[4]

Jammu and Kashmir and World War II

The war actually broke out on 1st September but its imminence was fairly clear by 23 Aug.[5] Reacting to the tense situation in Europe, His Highness the Maharaja of Jammu and Kashmir sent the following telegram to His Excellency, the Viceroy of India on 24th August:

"Last night's wirelessed news sounded ominous, I hope I am wrong and must meet the resulting aggression on peace loving humanity and defend the sanctity of hearth and home and the cause of honour. I deprecate publicity but I desire Your Excellency and through you the kind

Emperor to know that if the war comes, Jammu and Kashmir may be depended upon to do what Jammu and Kashmir has ever done since coming under the aegis of his Britannical Majesty, and of course my personal services are always and will be, in the event of war, at His Majesty's disposal".[6]

Simultaneously, he placed two units of the state forces at the disposal of His Excellency, the Viceroy, and issued instructions to all officers and soldiers, who were on leave, to report to their respective units. The Infantry Battalions and Batteries were also kept in readiness to move at short notice.[7]

Maharaja's anticipatory action had been so fast that the day after the war actually broke out, all the units of the state forces stood mobilised for war and in a state of readiness to march out in a short notice. All these units were then placed at the disposal of the British Government. He appealed to every Indian that India must stand shoulder to shoulder with England in this hour of emergency. The settlement of their political differences must wait for the return of peace.[8]

Jammu and World War II

Not more than two decades after the termination of the 1st world war, the people of Jammu region got another opportunity to prove their valour, when the state forces mobilised to help the Allies in the Second World War.[9]

Maharaja made an impassioned appeal to the Dogras in general and Rajputs in particular to help in the war effort by enrolling themselves in the army either in the state or in the Indian army.[10] In order to induce the people to lend whole hearted support to the cause, his appeal was supplemented by the following proclamation issued by his Govt.[11] *"His Highness, Maharaja Bahadur with his unfailing regard for his subjects in general and the army in particular has been graciously pleased to order that the officers and men of the units of his army, who may sent on active service shall continue to receive their pay and rations allowance from the state."*

As field rations and other field requirements are sure to be provided by the British Government.

His Highness had ruled that the state shall not save the ration allowance but during the absence of the units from the state, pay that allowance to the families of those who are in active service and such payments shall continue until the mobilised units remain in service outside the state. To encourage the recruitment, he assured everyone and said,

"Let every man who may here after enlist under His Highness's "Banner" realise that when he goes to fight at the bidding of his master, he does so as a soldier of a sovereign who will not only look after him, while he is on the battle field, but also look after his family, and if should he loose his life, his master will in the absence of the bread winner, not leave his family uncared for".[12]

Through the same proclamation, the families of all those men serving outside the state were given a "family allowance of Rs. six a month, in addition to their pay and ration allowance from the state exchequer".[13]

"So far as those who are already serving in some unit or the other of His Highness Army, let themselves and their families take heart that the master who may order them to go and fight, will make it as his case to do all that is possible not to allow their families to suffer destitution or involved in abject poverty".[14]

The Maharaja, in a message to his state forces, conveyed to them: "You go attend by my good wishes. All the time you are away, you will be in my thoughts I trust you to give a good account of your self, such an account as will add glory to the state and bring honour to yourself. Good luck and God be with you."[15]

In order to give the proclamation wide publicity, one lakh copies of it were printed in Urdu, of those 750 were distributed among the press correspondents, newspapers, institutions and persons on the government's mailing list, while 73,000 and 26,000 copies were distributed in the province of Jammu and Kashmir respectively. [16]

The response to the Maharaja's appeal was tremendous and right through the period of war, there never was a dearth of recruits for not only the state forces but also the Indian army. The Amar Sabha of Jammu, through a telegram, offered their loyal and united services to His Highness in the conduct of war. Some individuals, too, offered their services to their Maharaja for the righteous cause, whereas many pensioners offered their services without any extra emoluments. [17]

Similarly, the Wazir of Poonch, through his telegram sought to convey the feelings of Poonch. Poonch people were eager for enlistment in Indian and State Armies. *"Kindly wire number of Hindus and Muslim recruits required from Poonch for emergency and other recruitments. Poonch can supply over ten thousand recruits."*[18]

On September 18th, 1939, the Jammu and Kashmir Praja Sabha (legislative assembly), while endorsing the Maharaja's appeal, resolved.

The Praja Sabha, representing all classes, communities and interests in the state, expresses its unflinching devotion to Your Highness and support whole-heartedly and unreservedly Your Highness' determination to offer all the resources of the state, both in men and material, in the furtherance of the righteous causes, in which the armies of His Majestry, the King Emperor are engaged, namely, the cause prevalence of right over might and upholding the reign of law over brute force." [19]

This time the people of this region responded better than during the previous war, and nearly 51,000 recruits joined the army (Indian Army 45,000, state forces 6,000) upto the end of 1943.[20] By the end of the war total number of the recruits raised from Jammu region was about 55,000.[21] Considering the total population of Jammu province was a little over 40,00,000, which included women, children, the old and infirm and a large section of the non-martial races. In response to these efforts, more persons with higher physical standards came forward to join the army. They include the Sikhs, Gujjars and Jats as well.[22]

The working committee of the National Conference declared its support to the war efforts of the state government but it also showed resentment over the special appeal made by the Maharaja to the Dogras and the Rajputs in the state to support the allied war efforts, ignoring rest of the people of the state. No doubt, the National Conference was justified in showing its resentment, as the appeal had been made only to the Dogras and Rajputs of the state. According to them, the people of Kashmir, too, had every opportunity to contribute towards the war afforts of the state.[23]

The working committee of the National Conference on 16th and 18th May, 1942 issued the following statement.

"At this juncture of the world history, it is high time that the people should realise the significance of the increasing danger to our country from the world's fascist forces. People must be roused from their apathetic attitude towards this war, which in the opinion of the working committee is no more a purely imperialistic conflict but has changed into people front of their entire world against the fascism and reaction, no matter that reaction is of home-made variety or of a foreign brand, the people of the state, Kashmir, too, have every opportunity to contribute towards the war efforts of the state."[24]

In J&K, 1st J & K Mountain Battery, formed a part of the 5th Indian Division which was mobilised for service overseas. It was under the command of Lt Col Baghwan Singh. It distinguished itself in the conquest of Eritres, particularly in the battle of Keren and capture of Asmara, as well as in the invasion of Syria, where it won great battle honours on account of its gallant part in the attack on Jebel Mazar (Damascus).[25]

The 2nd J&K Mountain Battery and Four Infantry Battalions served on the north western frontier of India. After serving there for four years, The 4th J & K Infantry was sent to Burma to join the 5th Indian Division. There it earned great battle honours in the famous advance from Tiddin and in the attacks on vital corner, Kennedy Peak and Fort While.[26]

The commander of the Division, with which the battery served, praised the standard of its efficiency under skilled command of Lt Col Bhagwan Singh Similarly, General Sir Claude Aruchinleck, C-in-C of the Imperial forces in the Middle East, conveyed his personal appreciation of the work of the battery to His Excellency Archibald Wavell, C-in-chief of India (Later H.E., Lord Wavell, the Viceroy of India who, while adding his own appreciation, conveyed it to His Highness the Maharaja of Jammu and Kashmir. It said:

"J&K Battery acquitted itself with great distinction in recent Damascus fighting. Divisional Commander commends its steadiness under the enemies artillery fire and the accuracy of its own fire supporting British Infantry".[27]

Maharaja on receiving the message of appreciation, felt elated and sent the following message to Lt Col Bhagwan Singh in appreciation of his heroic deeds.

"Your Divisional Commander, also General Aruchinleck and the C-in-C in India have expressed their appreciation of the work of your self your officers in Damascus; remarked that you all acquitted yourselves

with great distinction. I am most proud of you, and greatly value the fine example you set for your brother officers and men of all other units in the field, well done. My best wishes for your further success in the future".[28]

In recognition of services of Lt Col Bhagwan Singh, the Maharaja on 20 Dec., 1941 sanctioned a hereditary *Jagir* of Rs 3,600 per annum in his favour, which could be held by him and his male heirs in the direct line perpetuity.[29]

On October 1st, 1942, both the Mountain Batteries, i.e., first and second, serving outside the state and the Artillery training centre were incorporated as permanent units with the Indian Army.[30] During the transfer, however, every care was taken by the state government to protect the service conditions and professional interests of the soldiers. Those who could not be retained in the Indian army at the end of the war were to be eligible for concessions authorised for regular pre-war units of the Indian army.[31]

Awards

For conspicuous gallantry, while serving in the various fields of the war, following decorations and honours were won by the valiant sons of this region.[32]

Decorations	*No. of Decoration won*
1. Victoria Cross	One
2. Military Cross	Five
3. Distinguished Flying	One
4. Indian Order of Merit	Two
5. Indian Distinguished Service Medals	Fifteen
6. Member of the Br Empire British	Seven
7. Military Medal	Fortyone
8. Order of the Br Empire (Military)	One
9. Order of the Br India	Five
10. M.B.E. (Military)	Two[33]

The demand for the Dogras in general and for the Dogra Rajput particularly had vastly increased. Accordingly, full recruiting facilities were provided to the Government of India. [34]

In order to moralise public, a War Aid Committee was organised in July, 1940 under the presidentship of Her Highness, the Maharani Sahiba. The committee established its branches in every tehsil all over the state.[35] The aim of these committees was to collect funds in aid of the war and to disseminate correct information regarding the happening on the front.[36]

In addition to the collecting of funds, the War Aid Committee also organised working parties twice a weak, where participants had to prepare garments, scarfs, hand-kerchief, bandages, etc. for the use of soldiers deployed on the front.[37] The services of hospital staff and private medical practitioners were also secured for the production of some essential medical articles.[38] A number of government and private industries, too, occupied themselves in the manufacture of articles required by the supply department of the Government of India.[39]

The War Aid Committee also established the *"Triket Tund."* The contribution received by the committee till the end of February, 1945 was Rs 9,87,315, which included Rs 2,50,440 from the ruling family itself. The Maharaja Hari Singh contributed the additional sum of Rs 2,79,47 from his own privy purse. The private individuals, revenue officer, jagirdars and lambardars had public meetings to persuade the people to make contribution for war.[40]

The war years saw the scarcity of food stuffs and other essentials of life. People saw untiring efforts on the part of the leaders to prevent black marketing by unscrupulous dealers in these commodities. The war years also saw the growing importance of the Maharaja with the British

Government.[41] He gave unstinted help to, and placed all his resources at the disposal of the Government of India in their prosecution of the war. Any action that he would take against the people movement received support from the imperial government.[42]

However, at national level, the Indian National Congress in its reaction to the declaration of India as Billegrant country without consulting Government of India, the Congress Ministers resigned forthwith. The Congress working committee met at Wardha and adopted the famous *'Quit India'* resolution. This resolution was accepted with some modification by the All India Congress Committee when it met in Bombay on 7th and 8th August, 1942.[43]

On 9th August, the Government of India swooped on the Congress rank and file. Gandhji and other Congress leaders were arrested.[44]

In response to the Quit India Movement the people of Jammu and Kashmir mounted a strong protest and demanded their release. In Jammu, students boycotted their schools and colleges, the offices and business centres were closed. They demanded that the reopening of negotiations for Indian Independence so the anti-fascist forces may be strengthened. At a number of places minor clashes occurred between the police and the students. A number of Congress supporters were arrested and imprisoned.[45]

Royal Commission, 1943

On 12th July, 1943, Hari Singh by a proclamation announced the appointment of a high power enquiry commission to look into the working of constitution of the state and the social and economic conditions of the state subjects.

The rulers instructed the commission to make recommendation for political reform and suggest measures for the economic upliftment of the people in the state.[46]

In the proclamation, Hari Singh declared that the people of all communities and all the faiths are equal. He pointed out that the commission had been appointed to make reommendations on the basis of which constitutional reforms could be introduced in the state, which would permit wider participation of the people in the state government and its administration.[47] The commission was constituted of twenty members.[48]

The Royal Commission was instructed to investigate conditions, needs and environment of the people of Jammu and Kashmir and suggest measures to secure the collective interest of the people as well as the welfare of the various communities and groups living in the state.[49]

The appointment of the commission evoked mixed reactions from the different political organisations in the state.[50] The National Conference, Yuvak Sabha, Hindu Rajya Sabha, the Congress Committee in Jammu and the Hindu Navjawan Sabha expressed satisfaction on the intentions of the ruler to introduce constitutional reforms in the state and take measures to ameliorate the economic conditions of the people.[51] The appointment of the enquiry commission was hailed as "a timely step in the direction of the political reforms and economic emancipation of the people in the state".[52] However, expressed disappointment at the constitutions of the commission and the predominance of the jagirdars, Pensioners, concession holders and officials of the government.[53]

The leaders of the Muslim Conference, however, severely criticised and disapproved the appointment of the Royal Commission. They were frustrated and angry at the inclusion of the representatives of the National Conference in the commission and not giving any representation to the Muslim Conference.[54]

The Royal commission of Enquiry was inaugurated on 9th August, 1943, with great pomp and show in the old palace of the Maharaja in Srinagar. Roy Bahadur Ganga Nath, the chairman of the commission read a message of the ruler. In his message, Hari Singh communicated: "If you work together, not in a narrow and mutually distrustful spirit, but with affixed resolve to serve the best interests of the state and in that loyalty on which I depended. I fell fully confident that your labour will be fruitful and add to the moral and material welfare of the inhabitants of the State".[55]

The commission invited minutes of references, memoranda and evidence from the general public and received considerable and detailed facts and data from various individuals and organisations, it did not carry on its deliberations in an atmosphere of trust and freedom. The chairman of the commission imposed a number of limitations and restrictions, *no* members so far as in the discussion and the debates in the commission were concerned. [56] The National Conference submitted a minute to the commission for its consideration. The minute underlined the reforms, the Conference sought to introduce in the state and among other measures included the introduction of responsible government institutions, freedom of press and speech, improvement of the standard of the living of the people and the remission of heavier taxes, ceases and duties.

Many of the members of the commission were not in any case interested in any political reform and therefore, did not allow the commission to deliberate upon such major issues, viz., the institutions of responsible government, the economic reorganisation, industrial and agricultural development, freedom of the press, platform and expression etc. that were raised by the members who represented the different organisations in the commission. Ganga Nath, particularly refused with the members of the commission, the permission to discuss the powers and position of the rulers, the ruling dynasty, army, judiciary, the Jagirs and the Private departments, Ganga Nath interpreted the terms of the reference for the way he deemed feasible.[57]

The National Conference leadership disapproved of manner in which the deliberations of the commission were conducted.[58] Gulam Mohammad Sadiq presented an elaborate report on the working of the commission to the working committee of the National Conference in the first week of February. The National Conference decided to recall its representative from the commission. Accordingly on 28th February, 1943, Gulam Mohammed Sadiq and Mirza Afzal Beg withdrew from the Commission of Inquiry. Thus, there was no representative left in the commission except secretaries, jagirdars and pro-government men.

Bread Agitation, 1943

Shortly after the inauguration of the Royal Commission, an agitation popularly known as *Roti agitation,* which was solely economic in nature occurred in the state in September, 1943. The main cause of the agitation was the rise in prices of the essential commodities and other items of daily use. The agitation was confined mainly to Jammu, the winter capital of the state and its surrounding areas. As mentioned above the Jammu region contributed in the war efforts of the government both in man and material. No doubt the people of Jammu region got the employment opportunities in Indian army, but the rise of essential commodities had naturalised all those concessions which their families were receiving from the state government.

S. No.	Particulars (per rupees)	Weight (in Ser) 1938	1940	1941	1942	1943
1.	Wheat	13-14	12-15	11-12	9	5-6
2.	Rice	10	5-6	4.75-6	3.5-6	4
3.	Maize Ghee (14 Chatak)	—	18	—	16	—
4.			64 Paisa	108 Paisa	112-120 Paisa	—
5.	Potato		8 Paisa	—	32 Paisa	—
	Fuel (Per manned)		—	28 Paisa	56.64 Paisa	—

The above Table is self-explanatory that the prices soared to nearly 400 per cent in respect of essential commodities, whereas in case of others it was between 12 per cent to 17 per cent. During the same period, the defence expenditure of the state also increased by 108 per cent, i.e., from Rs 49,16,700 to Rs 1,20,53,000, which was not only an unproductive expenditure but a huge burden on the state exchequer.

Realising the gravity of the situation, on 26th August, 1943, Dr Balram Das and Choudhary Hamid-ullah Khan, both members of the Praja Sabha wrote a letter to Rai Bahadur Himmat Singh, the then Revenue Minister. Almost during the same period, a deputation comprising S. Mool Singh Khosla, Advocate Lala Dina Nath Mahajan, Lala Shiv Nath Nenda, Sheikh Aziz Khan (all members of Praja Sabha), Sheikh Abdul Haj Dogra., *Vakil* Lala Rama Nath Balgotra (Editor *Dash Savek*) and Lala Mulk Raj Saraf (Editor *Ranbir*) waited on the Prime Minister Mr. Kaiiash Narain Haksar at Srinagar.

In the meeting, the Revenue Minister was also present. The deputations, too, raised the issue of rising prices and pressed upon the government to take action against hoarders and profiteers, arrangement for opening fair shops and storage of food grains at different places so that they could be released at appropriate time. The leading Urdu weekly, the Ranbir summarising the deliberations of the meeting not only cautioned the authorities about the consequences of the price hike but asked various organisations to fight the issue of rising of prices under a single platform.

Womenfolk are the worst suffers of the price rise, because they have to attend the food requirement of their family. Accordingly, the Istri Samaj had already started prabhat pheris to raise their concern against increase in prices. On 22nd September, 1943, a procession under the aegis of Public Relief Committee was organised. It was attended by 20,000 people from all walks of life. The processions marched towards Raghunath Chowk under the leadership of Lala Gopal Dutt Mengi raising slogans *"Hai Roti, Hai Roti", "Uttam Singh Mar Gaya, Himmat Singh* (Revenue Minister and Incharge Food and Supplies) *Mar Gaya*". The procession culminated at Mubarak Mandi where leaders made fiery speeches.

At the same time, National Conference, the Muslim Conference, Hindu Rajya Sabha and the Congress committee in Jammu constituted a joint front to fight the famine. On 22nd August, 1943, a week after the inauguration of Royal Commission of Enquiry, the front gave an ultimatum to the government to take immediate steps to improve the supplies of food grains in Jammu.[60] In order to pressurise the government, they organised demonstrations against the state government all over Jammu.

Kailash Narayan Haksar sent the Revenue Minister of the state, Himmat Singh, to Jammu to make an spot enquiry. Himmat Singh promised immediate help to the leaders of the joint front and returned to Srinagar.[61] However, no measures were taken to send succor to relieve the distress of the people in Jammu, thought the government had adequate reserves of food grains in the two provinces.[62]

The state administration did not like the various political organisations to politicise the situation in Jammu. The state government imposed a ban on all the processions under Rule 50 of the Jammu and Kashmir Defence Rules. Consequently, Lala Gopal Dutt Mengi and Kaviraj Vaishno Gupta along with others were arrested. At about 5 pm the news spread that the police had arrested Gopal Dutt Mengi, Kaviraj Vaishno Gupta. Bua Ditta, Mela Ram, Choudhary Noor Mohd, Choudhary Shehab Din and others. They were taken on foot via Purani Mandi to City Chowk. The arrest of the leaders caused a wave of resentment among the people in Jammu. The same afternoon, women of the city led a procession against the arrest of their leaders. This procession was followed by men in large numbers. They marched towards City Chowk where their leaders were kept; but they were not allowed to proceed to City Chowk. The police used lathi-charge on the processionists and situation was out of control.

Not only women but some police men were also injured. The Governor's car and a police van was also set on fire.[63]

The public demonstrations against the government continued unabated the next day. On 24th September, 1943, it was Jumat-ul-Vida (the last Friday of Ramzan), a large number of Muslims had assembled to offer prayer. In order to avoid any untoward happening, the Governor called for military assistance. On the morning, no incident was reported in the city. But in the evening, the citizens of Jammu organised a huge demonstration in defiance of the Defence Rules raising slogans, *"Hai Roti, Hai Roti"*. The procession passing through main *bazaars*, reached City Chowk via Kanak Mandi. The procession was led by five young men (two Hindus and three Muslims, who were garlanded and offered themselves for arrest. The processionists were chanting *"Hai Roti, Hai Roti"*, it was responded loudly from the crowd and its echo engulfed the whole city.

In response to the slogans, people came out from their houses, and gathered near Old Hospital Road (now Super *Bazaar*). The police had already erected barriers to stop the movement of civilians. The magistrate on duty ordered people to disperse but people stuck to their place. Consequently, a clash took place which was followed by police firing, on the agitators. In this incident of firing eight people were killed out of which six were Hindus and two Muslims.

At the same time, curfew was imposed in the city. During the midnight of September 24th and 25th, a total of 32 arrests were made. On 25th September, the funeral procession of the dead was arranged by the people in which over 25,000 people participated. The funeral procession was a symbol of unity between the two major communities. The Muslim carried the dead bodies of Hindus and recited *"Ram Ram"* whereas Hindus carried the dead bodies of Muslims and chanted *"Allah Allah"*. The mortal remains of those killed were cremated/laid to rest at the same place.

Maharaja Hari Singh was shocked to receive the news. He directed that the Praja Sabha session due on 25th September be adjourned. Meanwhile, Rai Bahadur Justice Ganga Nath took the oath as the new President of the Praja Sabha, therefore read the Maharaja's order and adjourned the house.

In Srinagar, people, too, observed complete *hartal* to express their solidarity with people of Jammu, where as Choudhery Ghulam Abbas of Muslim Conference and S. Budh Singh from National Conference personally conveyed their heart felt condolences to the bereaved families.

Sheikh Mohammad Abdullah directed his colleagues. Mirza Afzal Beg and Khawaja Ghulam Mohammad Sadiq. to proceed to Jammu and submit a report regarding the happening in Jammu. While Mirza Yousuf Shah demanded strict action regarding the happening. Similar sentiments were aired by Muslim Student's Federation.

On the instructions of Maharaja Hari Singh, the Prime Minister Sir Kailash Narayan Haksar and Revenue Minister Rai Bahadur Himmat Singh reached Jammu in 27th September. They were accompanied by Parliamentary Secretary and Pandit Prem Nath Dogra, Dr Balram Dass, Lala Shiv Nath Nanda and Sheikh Mohammad Amin. They conducted a survey of *bazaars* and took stock of the occurrences of the events. They also met the members of Public Relief Committee and submitted their report to the Maharaja at Srinagar. The ministers assured would an inquiry would be conducted and pubic demands will be addressed accordingly.

It was on their assurances the *hartal* was called off. The city, which remained under *hartal* for consecutive nine days, opened itself to business. It was estimated the traders suffered a loss of one lakh rupees. [64]

However, Maharaja Hari Singh ordered two hundred thousand maunds of rice to be rushed from the adjoining township of Kathua to Jammu. The flour mills in Jammu city were taken over by the Governor of Jammu.[65] An enquiry committee to probe the incident of caning and firing on the mob was appointed. The Committee consisted of :

1. Hon'ble Sir Govind Madgavkar, Retired Judge Bombay High Court (Chairman) ;
2. Hon' ble B.K. Sen, Retired Judge, Patna High Court (Member);
3. Hon' ble Kazi Masud Hassan, Judge, J&K High Court.

The Committee after receiving representation submitted its report. The Committee not only consulted the officers involved in the incident but it also recommended a compensation of Rs 36,015 out of which Rs 22,420 was given to the kins of deceased and Rs 13595 to 18 injured in police firing.[66]

The Bread Agitation in Jammu and the consequent firing in Jammu town had senous repercussions in the Kashmir province. Mass meetings were held all over Srinagar against the police firing in Jammu. The food shortage was acute in Kashmir provinee as well and widespread demonstrations occurred in Srinagar and the other towns against firing in Jammu. The government moved in quickly, and ordered for the increase in the ration quota of the food grains and extended *"Ankoot"* distribution to the other townships of the province. Meanwhile Section 50 of the Defence of Jammu and Kashmir Rules was promulgated in Srinagar and processions and public meetings all over the province were prohibited. The Roti Agitation was purely of economic in nature.[67] The conspicuous fact of the agitation was that irrespective of the caste, creed and gender, destruction and their respective political affiliations joined hand together to fight for their basic right. This shows the people of Jammu region were becoming conscious of their rights.

New or Naya Kashmir

After the Roti Agitation, National Conference presented a new plan known as *Naya Kashmir* in 1944. Freda Bedi, an English women, who was associated with the National Conference suggested to the National Conference leaders to prepare a fresh and comprehensive plan for the national reconstruction and political reforms in the state.[68] The plans, originally prepared by Bedi in English, were translated into Urdu by Maulana Sayeed Masoodi, the General Secretary of the Conference.

The *"Naya Kashmir"* plan was presented by Sheikh Mohammad Abdullah to Maharaja Hari Singh in Srinagar in 1944. The plan which National Conference laid down was an all sided advancement along advances of human activity regulated in a democratic manner on a country wide scale. The plan covered agriculture, industry, transport, distribution of utility service, currency and the finance. The scheme was based on the "democratic principal of responsible government with the elective principal applied from the local panchayat right up to legislative assembly".[70] *"New Kashmir"* stirred the intellectuals of the state and become a burning topic both in Kashmir and Jammu province.

Dyarchy

In October, 1944, the ruler of the state, Maharaja Hari Singh, announced by a proclamation he had decided to appoint two ministers to this council from among the members of the Praja Sabha. The proclamation of the Ruler provided Praja Sabha would elect six members from among the elected members of the Sabha and would submit the panel of the members to elect the Ruler; consequently, the Ruler would appoint two ministers from the panel, one of whom would be a Muslim and the other a Hindu.[71] The ministers would function as a part of the council appointed by the Maharaja and were charged to administer matters which were transferred to them. They were responsible to the Maharaja and remained in office during his pleasure.[72]

Erroneously, the scheme, envisaged by the proclamation, came to be called "Dyarchy". On the recommendation of the Praja Sabha, Maharaja Hari Singh appointed Wazir Ganga Ram from Jammu region and Mirza Ahal Beg from Kashmir region.[73] The National

Conference accepting the dyarchy believed (a) it was a half-way towards responsible government and should, therefore, be given a trail; (b) while accepting the scheme, the National Conference would make it clear to the Ruler that the dyarchy did not satisfy the aspiration of the people. The Muslim conference, however, rejected the scheme out rightly.[74]

The people of Jammu region were not really losers. They got unprecedented employment opportunities in both the state and Indian army, which helped them to raise their standard of life and widened their mental horizon. They became fully conscious about their political and economic rights and their external influence also made them conscious.

The war years from (1939-1945) opened mixed opportunities for the people of the state. On the one hand, they got new opportunities of employment in Indian army both in combatant and non-combatant units. On the other hand, it gave fillip to the cottage industry in the state. The soldier, who participated shoulder to shoulder with the British army units, were intoxicated with the confidence that they were in no way inferior to British soldiers. It was because of this confidence they started giving vent to their feeling of political consciousness. Consequently, they and their families gave an overwhelming support of every agitation which concerned the rights and privileges of the people of the state.

References

1. Singh, Major, K. Brahma, *History of Jammu and Kashmir Rifles (1820 - 1956)*, Lancer International, New Delhi, p. 173.
2. Historical Section Ministry of Defence, *File No. 60117983/H, 1943*, p. 15.
3. *Ibid.*
4. Sharma, S.C., "*Maharaja Hari Singh's* contribution to World War II in "*Maharaja Hari Singh*" Edited by the M.L. Kapoor, Har-Anand Publication, New Delhi. 1995. p. 87.
5. *Ibid.*
6. G.O.I.P.D. (Pol. Branch), *File No. 40 (12) - (5)/3 of 1939*, p. 54, *Crown File No. 287 (N.A.I) War Efforts of Jammu and Kashmir*, p. 10, J & K I, Vol. 2, No. 3 Victory Number, May-June, 1954, p. 9.
7. *Jammu and Kashmir Information*, April 1944, p. 5, *Administrative Report Jammu and Kashmir 1938-39, Ibid.*, also S.C. Sharma op cit. p. 87.
8. G.O.I.R.D. (Pol. Branch) *File No. 40 (12)-(S)/39 of 1939*, 54, p. *Crown File No. 287 (N.A.I)* pp. 4 and *War Efforts of Jammu and Kashmir*, JKI, Vol. 2, No. 3, Victory Number, May-June, 1954, p. 9 and the *War, Maharaja of J&K, Personal Appeal*, September, 1939, p. 45.
9. *Ibid.*
10. *The War, Maharaja of J & K, Personal Appeal*, September, 1939, p. 45.
11. *Administrative Report, J&K, 1938-39*, pp. 210-215; Singh, Maj K. Brahma, *History of Jammu and Kashmir Rifles (1820-1956)*, p. 121; and *Crown file No. 287, (N.A.I) "The War Efforts to Jammu and Kashmir"*, J.K. Vol. 2, No. 3. Victory No. May-June, p. 9.
12. *Ibid.* also Sharma, S.C., op cit., p. 92.
13. *Ibid*, also Sharma, S.C., op cit., p. 92

14. *Ibid.*
15. *Administrative Report, 1992-93.* Also Sharma, S.C., op cit., p. 89.
16. *Ibid.*
17. Sharma, S.C., op cit., p. 88.
18. *Ibid.*
19. *Ibid* p. 86
20. *J.K.I.*, Vol. I, No. I, April 1944, p. 7, and *War Effort of Jammu and Kashmir State*", J.K., Vol. 2, No. 3, May-June 1945, p. 9.
21. Saraf, Mulk Raj, op cit., p. 171.
22. Singh, Maj. K. Brahma, *History of Jammu and Kashmir Rifles (1820-1906)*, p. 121.
23. *Praja Sabha Debates*, 21st April, 1941, p. 221, also Sharma, S.C., op. cit., pp. 88-89.
24. Dhar, D.N., p. 67, also Sharma, S.C., op cit., p. 99.
25. *Fortnight Report of Kashmir Residency* for the fortnight ending 31st January, 1942, GoI, *F.P.D File No. 9 (9)-P of 1942*, p. 5 and *crown file No. 287 (N.AJ)*, P. 21 and *Administration Report of the Army Deptt.* for Sumbat 1997-98 (1940-41) A.D., p. I and *War Efforts of Jammu and Kashmir State*-J&K, Vol. 2, No. 3, victory number, May-June 1945. pp. 10 and A *Hand Book of J&K State, 1947* p. 57.
26. *Administrative Report of the Army Deptt.* for Sumbat 1997-98 (1940-41) A.D., p. 1 and *Administrative Report of the Army Deptt.* for Sambat 2000 (1943-44 A.D), P. 1 and *Maharaja of Jaipur file no. 63*, pp. 66-67.
27. *Military Records*, Block A & B State Archive, Jammu, pp. 23-45, also Sharma, S.C., op. cit., p. 89 and Sharma, S.C, op. cit., p. 89.
28. *Ibid.*, p. 90.
29. *Ibid.*, also Sharma, S.C. op cit., p. 90.

30. *Ibid, Administrative Report 1943-44*, p. 61 and *A handbook of Jammu and Kashmir States*, G. J & K, Pub., 1947, p. 59.
31. Sharma, S.C. op cit., p. 90.
32. "*War Efforts of J&K States*", JK I, Vol., 2, No. 3. May-June, 1945, p. 18.
33. "War Efforts of Jammu and Kashmir State". JKI. Vol. 2, No. 3, May-June 1945, p. 18 and Saraf, Mulkh Raj. op. cit., p. 174
34. Sharma, S.C., op cit., p. 91.
35. Sharma, S.C., op cit., p. 93.
36. *Ibid.*
37. *Ibid.*
38. *Ibid*.
39. *Ibid.*
40. *Ibid., J & K Annual Administrative Reports 1945-46*, p. 395.
41. Koul, G. L., *Kashmir Then and Now-A Historical Survey*, Srinagar, 1967, p. 103.
42. Barnzai, P.N.K, *Cultural and Political History of Kashmir*. pp. 740-74.
43. Philips, C. H., *Evolution of India and Pakistan*, p. 32, New Delhi.
44. Alexander, H., *India since Crips*, New Delhi, p. 47.
45. *Martand*, Srinagar, 28th August, 1942, p. 9.
46. *Command order*, dated 12th July 1943, p. 2 and *Govt. Gazette*, 18th July 1943, p. 2 and *Proclamation* 66/H of 1943, p. 5.
47. *Ibid.*
48. *Ibid* and Hassnain, F. M, pp. 116-117.
49. *Statesment*, 22 July, 1943, *Royal Commission Enquiry Report*, p. 9.
50. *Ibid*., p. 10

51. Taseer, Rashid, *Tahreek Huryat Kashmir*, pp. 265-272.
52. *Ibid*.
53. *Dawn, Srinagar*, 19th July, 1943.
54. *Ibid*.
55. *Daily Herald*, 12th August 1943, p.7 and Koul, Santosh, *Freedom Struggle in Jammu and Kashmir*, p. 171.
56. *Report of Royal Commission*, p. 455, Jammu and Kashmir State Archives, Srinagar.
57. *Proceedings of the Working Committee of National Conference*, Khalid, Kashmir 3rd March, 1944, p. 122.
58. *Ibid.*
59. *Ibid.*
60. *Ibid.*
61. *Ibid.* and *Such*, Jammu, 11th April, 1966, p. 3.
62. *Ibid.*
63. *Ibid.*
64. *Ibid.*
65. *Ibid.*
66. Taseer, Rashid, *Tareek Huryat Kashmir*, p. 259.
67. *Report of the Inquiry Committee into Firing in Jammu*, 5th April 1944, p. 7.
68. *Resolution of Working Committee of the National Conference* 20th February, 1944, p. 45 and *Naya Kashmir*, Barnzai, Director of Information, New Delhi, Sec. 24.
69. *Ibid.*
70. *Ibid* and *Adm. Report 1943-45*, Part-II Sections 1, 2, 3, p. 392.
71. *Proclamation* 20th October, 1944, p. 72.
72. Tang, M.K., Koul and Koul, *Kashmir Constitutional History and Documents*. p. 157.

73. Khalid, Srinagar, 6th October, 1944, p. 3 and *Milat*, Srinagar, 27th October, 1944, p. 5.
74. *Proclamation,* 20th October, 1944, p. 72.

4

QUIT KASHMIR TO ACCESSION, 1946-1947

After the World War II, the political situation in the state had vastly changed. Independence was on the anvil and the Muslim League In India was trying to establish its justification for demanding the partition of the country on the basis of two nation theory. It was natural the Muslim majority of the state of Jammu and Kashmir should have received its utmost attention. Muslim League started its communal disturbance in Poonch, Kotli, Mirpur, Reasi and Rajouri in 1945. In 1946, these disturbances developed pronounced communal overtones in these areas.[1]

On 19th February, 1946, the British Prime-Minister, Clement Attlee, declared the British Government had decided to send special mission of cabinet ministers to India, to negotiate a settlement with Indian leaders. On 16th May, 1946, the cabinet mission announced its plan which the mission evolved for a future constitutional framework for India, i.e.,

1. The formation of one union of India, constituting British Indian provinces and the Indian states with power to deal with foreign affairs, defence and communications.
2. The establishment of an Executive and a Legislature of the representatives from the British Indian provinces and the Indian states.

3. The right of the provinces to organise themselves into groups, being entitled to determine the provincial subjects to be reserved for a group.
4. The right of the provinces to claim, by a majority of their assembly votes, a revision of the constitutional provisions after on interval of every ten years.
5. Retention of the residuary powers by the province.
6. Opinion for the states to acede to the union.

On the 2nd May, 1946, Sheikh Mohammad Abdullah attended the State People Conference at Delhi on the cabinet mission proposals. There he issued a statement in which he pleaded for the repudiation of the treaty rights and claimed consideration for the right of the people of the state to self-determination. He demanded for a responsible government in Jammu and Kashmir state. His demand was not accepted and returned to Srinagar on 3rd May, 1946.[3] The Cabinet Mission's reference to the paramouncy issue provoked Sheikh Mohammad Abdullah, the leader of the National Conference in Kashmir, to challenge the validity of the treaty of Amritsar under obligation of which, paramouncy was to revert to Maharaja of Kashmir after the departure of British Government from India.

On 6th May, 1946, Shiekh Mohammad Abdullah addressing a public meeting at Srinagar lashed out at the state government for its duplicity and its attempt to undermine the movement for self-government in the state.[4] On 15th May, 1946, in other public speech at Srinagar, he launched what was termed as the *"Quit Kashmir"* movement.[5]

Quit Kashmir

Sheikh Mohammad Abdullah launched the Quit Kashmir Movement on the pattern of Quit India Movement without understanding whether there was any similarity of cause between the two. The Quit India

Movement was aimed to make the foreign rulers Quit from India, whereas in case of quit Kashmir, it was aimed at overthrowing the Maharaja, who was a son of the soil.

The Quit Kashmir movement was a total reversal of the earlier policy of the National Conference seeking a responsible government under the Maharaja as the constitutional monarch as envisaged in the "New Kashmir" concept of 1944.

On 14th May, 1946, Sheikh Mohammad Abdullah delivered a fiery speech at Nowshera, Srinagar where he said *"Kashmir has been sold by one traders to other. Gulab Singh purchased Kashmir and deceived the Sikh. Since the day of purchase, we have been treated like animals. National Conference aims at the termination of Dogra Shahi"*[7]

Next day, Sheikh Mohd Abdullah outlined the objectives of the Quit Kashmir Movement and called upon the people to prepare for last battle with the Dogra's.[8] On 16th May, 1946, Sheikh Mohd, Abdullah delivered a speech at Maisuma Srinagar, he said, *"In 1846, Gulab Singh committed detestable and now in 1946, it was obtained that I should reign by protest against it. We do not want to become victims of the pleasure of* Rajas, Maharajas *and* Nawabs. *A time will come when even the dead would emerge from graves raising slogans, "Dogra-Raj–Murda-bad–Kashmir–Ko–Chood–Do".*

He further said, "when the Indian freedom movement demands the complete withdrawal of British-power and restore sovereignty to its real owners, the people and when we raised the slogan Quit Kashmir, we naturally visualise that the prince and nawabs should quit all the states, i.e., state like Hyderabad. Every man, woman and child will shout Quit Kashmir."

The Quit Kashmir Movement spread like wild fire in different parts and created a bitter reaction against the Maharaja. During day and night slogans were heard:

"Dogra Raj Murdabad' "Hari Singh Hun Buol, Khudayan Gool". "Ramahoon Un Mool Zina Badli Zool"[10]

The Quit Kashmir Movement went on for some day in the form of speeches and slogans. The Quit Kashmir movement expressed its full agreement, on behalf of the people of the states, with the fresh resolution of the Constituent Assembly of India, which declared its firm and solemn resolve to proclaim India an Independent and sovereign Republic. It welcomed in particular, the declaration in regard to social, economic and political justice to all people of India, equality of status and opportunity before law and fundamental rights and safeguards for minorities, tribal areas and depressed and backward classes.

The Conference specially referred to the states of Kashmir (Jammu and Kashmir) and Hyderabad, reiterating its stand that nor the Indian states, including Kashmir and Hyderabad were part of India. The Conference stated, "An impression is, however, sought to be created in the minds of the people at large that Kashmir and Hyderabad can exist as independent entities on the termination of British power. The Conference wishes to make it clear that Kashmir and Hyderabad as also the other Indian states cannot be allowed to remain outside the orbit of independent India much less can they be allowed to determine the internal constitutional structure without the sanction of their people. Such an attempt, it must clearly be understood, will always be resented by the people and if necessary even resisted. [8]

Along with the other princely states, Jammu and Kashmir was also released from the operation of the British Paramouncy. Maharaja Hari Singh followed a policy of abiding time till power was transferred in Indian hands because Maharaja was dreaming of an independent Jammu and Kashmir state and another reason was that from all states here the Muslims were in majority and the ruler was a Hindu, so the ruler had to decide taking in all aspects into consideration. Thirdly, the ruling Congress party under the leadership of Jawahar Lal Nehru was out to support Sheikh Abdullah over the issue of accession.[9]

Meanwhile, the Maharaja was subjected to pressure from different direction to accede to India. The Congress leaders were not happy with the strange attitude of Jammu and Kashmir ruler towards National Conference. Political pressure on Maharaja by the Congress to accede to India began with the visit of Acharya Kripalani. [23]

Visit of Kriplani, Mountbatten and Gandhiji to J&K

In May 1941, the Congress leadership decided to send the Congress president, Acharya Kriplani, to Kashmir to make an assessment of the political situation and also try to persuade the ruler and the state government to adopt a policy of reconciliation towards the National Conference. [10]

The Hindus and the Sikhs entertained the hopes the visit of Acharya Kriplani would lead to a settlement of the existing crises in the state. [11] Acharya Kriplani reached Srinagar in the evening of May, 1947.

Kripalani said, "The freedom of India was near and the people of the Indian states would also get their freedom with the freedom of the Indian people." He said the Congress supported the National Conference for the freedom of the people of Jammu and Kashmir state. He also met the Maharaja and tried to persuade him to come to a settlement with the National Conference. [12] Hari Singh refused to accept an agreement with the National Conference. The Ruler also remained evasive with regard to the accession of the state to the Constituent Assembly.[13]

On 19th June, 1947, Lord Mountbatten visited Kashmir and remained there for four days. [14] He wanted to persuade

Maharaja and his Prime Minister Ram chand lal to make up their mind before 14th August, 1947.[15] Mountbatten in his speech said, "I persisted with the same advice, as certain with the will of your people by and means and join whichever dominion your people wish to join by 14th August, 1947". Maharaja told Mountbatten he did not want to accede to Pakistan on any account nor wish to join India but stay independent.[17]

On his return from Kashmir, Mountbatten not only had a detailed discussion with Nehru in regard to Kashmir, but he also sent a report of detailed discussion with Nehru to the Britishn Government. [18]

On 1st August, 1947, Gandhi visited Kashmir. He met Maharaja and his wife. He also met Abdullah and his close associate Bakshi Gulam Mohammad. Gandhi told Hari Singh frankly his subjects were predominantly Muslims and it would be in his interest to establish an atmosphere of trust in the state. Gandhi advised Hari Singh to establish a representative government in the state without any loss of time.[32] The outcome of Gandhi's visit was the removal of Ram Chand Kak and appointment of former Revenue Minister Janak Singh as the Prime Minister in his place.[19]

Independence of India

On the 14th August, 1947, the dominion of Pakistan was created and next day on 15th August, 1947, India became independent. At the partition of India, the Punjab and N.W.F.P. were not only engulfed with communal carnage, but a systematic campaign of murder and abduction was engineered against Hindus and Sikhs. [20]

As the fate of Gurdaspur district was yet to be decided by the Punjab Boundary Commission. The minority communities, realising they would be safe in a Hindu "Ruler's" state. Obviously, they started pouring in through Jammu and Hazara borders. By first quarter of 1947, about 60,000 and 25,000 refugees entered Jammu and Muzaffarabad respectively.[21]

Maharaja, however, made strenuous efforts to prevent the Punjab and N.W.F.P. violence from spilling over into his state. These developments decidedly forced Hari Singh to move very consciously and prolong his independence as long as possible.[22]

Independence of India

Hari Singh had a very close view of forming a state on the basis of religion meant for minorities. However, he was aware of the fact that state's commerce and trading links were with West Punjab (new Dominion of Pakistan). In the absence of the Punjab Boundary Commission award, the state had no direct link with east Punjab except Bhadarwah-Chamba road which was not workable. This forced the Maharaja to offer standstill agreements both to India and Pakistan.

The Government of India did not accept the standstill agreement and instead asked the ruler to depute a properly accredited representative of the state to discuss the implication of the standstill agreement. Whereas Pakistan accepted the standstill agreement offered by the ruler of the state.

The ink of the standstill agreement had yet not even dried, Pakistan started pressurising the Maharaja to accede to Pakistan. All entry points were sealed and not a drop of petrol and a grain of salt was allowed to enter the state.[23] At the same time, men in uniform were provoked to revolt against their ruler. This was followed by an invasion by Pak regular army in the guise of tribals. Thus, the Jammu and Kashmir, too, came in the grip of communal frenzy.

By the end of October 1947, after capturing the frontier areas, the half of the Poonch Jagir, the districts of Mirpur, Muzaffarabad and Baramulla, the invaders were just knocking at the doors of Srinagar, the summer capital of the state. Realising the emergency of the situation, the Maharaja on October 26th, 1947, signed the instrument of accession.

So, after the second world war, Independence was on the anvil. In 1946, Muslim Conference started "Quit Kashmir" movement against Maharaja the son of soil. But this movement failed. Mountbatten advised the Maharaja to join whichever dominion he liked, i.e., India or Pakistan. But the Maharaja did not want to join any dominion and wanted to remain Independent. This resulted in the invasion of Pakistan invaders from frontier side and compelled Maharaja to accept Indian accession on 26th October, 1947.

References

1. Singh, Major K. Brahma, *History of Jammu and Kashmir Rifles, 1822-1956*, New Delhi, p. 15.
2. *Ibid.*, p. 18.
3. *Statement presented by National Conference to the Cabinet Mission*, 2, May, 1946, Published by General Secretary National Conference, *Martand,* 24th April, p. 9.
4. J & K Archive, *File No. 506 of 1946*, p. 7 and *Hamdard*, Srinagar, 8th May, 1946, p. 2.
5. J & K Archive, *File No. 305 of 1946*, p. 3 and *Kidmat*, Srinagar, 9th May, 1944, p. 9.
6. *Statement of S. Mohd Abdullah, Ranbir Press*, 29th April, 1946 and Lt Col Bhagwan Singh, *Political Conspiracies of Kashmir*, pp. 3.
7. J & K Archive, Pol. Deptt., *File No. 607 of 1946*, pp. 3 -10, and *Statement of Sheikh Mohd Abdullah, Ranbir*, 29th April, 1946, p. 8.
8. *Kidhmat*, Srinagar, 11th May, 1946, p. 3 and *Hamdard*, Srinagar, 11th May, 1946, p. 5.
9. *Hamdard*, Srinagar, 11th May, 1946, p. 7, and *Kidmat*, Srinagar, 11th May, 1946, p. 10 and statement of Sheikh Mohd. Abdullah, *Ranbir* 29th April, 1946, p. 5.
10. J&K, Archive, Pol. Deptt., *File No. 209, 1946*, pp. 2-9, and *Ibid*.
11. *Ibid.*, and *Tribune* Srinagar, 26th May, 1946, p. 7.
12. *Ibid.*
13. *Khalid*, Srinagar, 24th May, 1946, p. 4 and *Hamdard*, Srinagar, 24th May, 1946, p. 9.
14. Statement Srinagar, 12th June, 1946, p. 75.
15. *Ibid.*
16. *Ranbir*, Jammu, p. 5.

17. Phillips, C.H., *Evolution of Pakistan*, p. 39 and Mansergh, Nichalar, *The Transfer of Power*, Vol. VII, p. 523, New Delhi.
18. Singh, Lt Col Bagwan, *Political Conspiracies of Kashmir*, p. 46.
19. *Ibid*.
20. *Ibid.*, p. 45.
21. *Ibid*.
22. J & K Archive, Pol. Deptt., File No. 32 of 1947, pp. 5-9.
23. *All India State Peoples Conference Papers*, Nehru Museum, 51, Part II, pp. 148-183, *File No. 8*, Part II, pp. 383.

5

RESPONSE TO NEW REALITIES, 1948-1953

The holocaust following partition brought untold miseries on the people of the state and those refugees of west Punjab who had come to their relatives and acquaintances in the state, with a hope that when the dust settled down they would return to their homes. Officially, 1,58,000 persons (excluding those who migrated from west Punjab) were registered as refugees from POK, occupied part of Jammu and Kashmir, while many other living close to the affected areas had shifted to safer p!aces among their friends and relatives.[1]

The areas annexed by Pakistan had not only deprived the state of its territories and uprooted millions of people, but its commercial links with outer world were completely snapped. The trade had a sorrow effect on the ability of all those living on or near the trade route to earn their livelihood. The worst sufferers were the people of Laddakh and Kargil tehsils. The market of Leh through which all the trade used to pass was now a pitiful reminder of happiness and prosperous times . Similarly, in Jammu region, the towns of Poonch, Akhnoor, Samba and Hiranagar were not only richest towns of the state but were considered an emporium of trade. But the partition had relegated them into oblivion.[2]

On 28th October, a day after the accession of the state, Maharaja Hari Singh appointed an emergency administration headed by Sheikh Mohammad Abdullah. The other leaders of the Conference were appointed as emergency officers in the emergency administration and were given the charge of various departments of the state government. Maharaja retained his council of ministers intact and the emergency administration was required to function under the supervision of the ruler and his ministry.[3]

The dual government did not work well. The National Conference demanded the appointment of a ministerial council for the state among the leaders of the National Conference and headed by the Sheikh Mohammad Abdullah.[4]

For some time, Hari Singh refused to consider any proposal which envisaged the appointment of a ministerial council composed of the Conference leaders. After long negotiations which were initiated by the government of India, an *interim* arrangement was made and an *interim* government headed by the Sheikh Mohammad Abdullah was constituted on 5th March, 1948. Almost all powers of the state government were entrusted to the *interim* government.

The new council of ministers consisted of Baks Gulam Mohammad, Mirza Afzal Beg, Khawaja Gulam Mohammad Sadiq, Pt Sham Lal and Sardar Budh Singh. In this new council of ministers, all members were from Kashmir except S. Budh Singh. The replacement of a Hindu Prime Minister, Meher Chand Mahajan, by Sheikh Mohd Abdullah and the composition of his cabinet developed a feeling of insecurity among the people of Jammu.[6]

Within a year after the formation of the *interim* government, Maharaja Hari Singh abdicated his throne and the Dogra rule virtually reached its end. At the same time, doings of National Conference government under Sheikh's leadership brought the people of Jammu into a direct confrontation with it.[7]

The people of Jammu wanted the Maharaja to be the head of the state wielding wide prerogative and powers in the case of emergency so that Muslim majority did not do whatever they like. They felt if National Conference remained unchecked, they would destroy Hindu culture and would ruin the Hindu minority in the state in many ways. Then they approached the Congress leaders so that they could find immediate redressal. But they found no encouragement from them.[8]

A feeling of discontent was growing among the Jammu people against Sheikh Mohammed Abdulah's rule because of his anti-Jammu and anti-monarchial attitudes. This brought a chasm between the National Conference government under Sheikh Mohammed Abdullah and the people of Jammu.[9]

Every person in Jammu region seemed to worry about the leaderless Jammu. The people of Jammu, thus, wanted a political organisation, which could reflect their aspirations and represent their viewpoints both at national and state level. This need was fulfilled by the birth of Praja Parishad. [10]

Origin and Growth of Praja Parishad

The people of Jammu were in need of a political organisation which could reflect their aspirations and respect their viewpoints in the changed political scenario. This need was met with the formation of the Praja Parishad in Jammu on 25th November 1947.[11] It was formed by a group of dissident R.S.S. workers, Mr Hari Wazir was its President and Mr. Balraj Modhak the General Secretary. The others were Prem Nath Dogra, Lala Rup Lal Nanda[12] (advocate). This organisation took up the cause of Jammu's identity and created political consciousness among the people of the state, particularly of Jammu region, who till then had remained loyal to the Maharaja, to prepare them for playing their proper role in the rapidly changing political situation in the state.[13]

The main object of this organisation was to achieve full integration of Jammu and Kashmir with India and raised the slogan *of Ek Nishan, Ek Vidhan and Ek Pradhan* and to safeguard their legitimate democratic rights of the people of Jammnu and anti-Dogra policies of Sheikh Mohammad Abdullah.[14]

Meanwhile, the Sheikh Abdullah administration passed the *Big Landed Estates Abduction Act in 1950.* This alienated increasingly a large number of Hindus in the state. The most controversial aspect of the programme was the sweeping revision of the state's land tenure system, abolishing several privileged farms of land handing. It was but natural that many of those deprived from their holding turned to Praja Parishad for the redressal of their frustration.[15]

The formation of Praja Parishad was not only welcomed but it emerged as an authentic voice of the people of Jammu.[16] It started its activities with an agitation from ending 1948. During the brief period of five years from its formation in 1947, the Praja Parishad waged three main movements in the years 1948-49, 50-51, 52-53.[17]

The Praja Parishad party considered Jammu and Kashmir state to be an inseparable and indivisible part of India. It aimed at establishing a political, social and economic order, in which there would be no discrimination on account of caste, colour and faith and the means and opportunity of progress would be provided to every individual without any gender bias.[18]

Activities and Struggle for Praja Parishad, 1948-49

After the accession with Indian Union, it was expected the fundamental unity of Jammu and Kashmir with the rest of India would be further strengthened by the adoption of a common constitution, a common law, a common flag and a common national language.[19] But what happened was quite opposite. Although, Sheikh Abdullah was loyal to India, he never lost right of what is known as the "Third Option"– that of Independence. Following the third option, the school going children were taught to consider Kashmir a nation in itself and India was described in their text books as a friendly neighbour. The insistence on having a separate flag, a separate constitution and a separate President was all that" inculcated a feeling of separate nationhood among the Kashmiris.[20] This aggressive attitude of the state government and hate campaign against the people of Jammu had its reaction. Thus, for the further safety and security of Jammu and Kashmir with which the safety and security of India was linked, Praja Parishad thought it essential the state should be fully integrated with Indian Union.[21]

In February 1949, there was the first clash between the National Conference government and Praja Parishad. The Praja Parishad organised a mass rally in Jammu city.[22] The Sheikh's government retaliated and hundreds of people along with Pt Prem Nath Dogra, the then President of Praja Parishad were arrested. For the first time, people of Jammu for setting any caste distinetions came under the banner of Praja Parishad.

Out of 195 *satyagrahi*, 45 women were arrested. Praja Parishad became one important popular political party of the Jammu region.[23]

Pt Prem Nath Dogra was the principal figure of the Praja Parishad party and was widely respected in the state. The Praja Parishad party expressed Jammu's discontent and wanted full accession of the state to Indian union and abrogation of Article 370 of Indian constitution that guaranteed it a special status.[24] Article 370 of the Indian constitution recognised the right of the people of the state to convene a constituent assembly of their own to draft the constitution of the state. This article envisaged an absolute limitation on the application of the provisions of The Constitution of India to the state. This made Sheikh Mohammed Abdullah increasingly autocratic and Sheikh Mohammad Abdullah reacted to full accession of the state to the Indian union and abrogation of article 370 of the Indian constitution. However, the agitation was suspended on the interventation of some of the prominent members of the Indian parliament. All the leaders of the Praja Parishad were released. Despite mass arrests, the fire of discontent kept smoldering in the hearts of people of Jammu.[25]

The Indian constitution was adopted on 26th January, 1950 recognising the right of the people of the state to convene a constituent assembly of their own, to draft the constitution for the state.[26] Sardar Patel the then Dy. P.M. and minister in-charge for states, made a statement in the Indian constituent assembly, "In view of the special problem the Jammu and Kashmir Government faced, we have made special provisions for the continuance of the state with the union on existing basis." [27] He further said "The existing bases were the basis of instrument of accession and the special provisions were embodied in Article 370 of The Constitution of India, which was to be a temporary provision in the constitution". It means that the state though an integral part of India, had special status in Indian constitution. [28]

Praja Parishad from the very beginning opposed the idea of granting special status to the state in accordance with the Article 370. The party not only presumed the finality of accession but also demanded an end to the privileged treatment of the state as provided in the Indian constitution. It was clear to the party President Pt Prem Nath Dogra and his colleagues that accession would mean little or nothing to the people of Jammu region as long as the state retained a special status under Article 370. [29] They were equally critical of the double talk of the National Conference leaders, who on one hand demanded secularism for the people in India and on the other hand insisted upon separate Muslim identity in Jammu and Kashmir. [30]

Enraged by the reaction of Jammuites against the special status, Sheikh Mohd Abdullah in one of his speech said, "If the people of Jammu, sincerely desire separation and establish an Independent Dogra Desh. I would say with full authority on behalf of Kashmiris that they would not at all mind this separation". This obviously revealed the mindset of Kashmiri leadership. The reaction of Sheikh Mohammad Abdullah revealed he would never like to discuss the problem of Jammu.[31] It is, therefore, natural that the trends such as revivalism, economic dissatisfaction and political uncertainty resulted in strengthening the hold of Praja Parishad in Jammu region.[32]

Praja Parishad Agitation from (1950-1951)

Election and Praja Parishad's Reaction and its Repression

Article 370 of the constitution empowered the people of the state to have their own constituent assembly. Accordingly on 30th April, 1951, Karan Singh, the Regent, issued a proclamation to order the convocation of the constituent assembly of the state. The Constituents Assembly was to be constituted of members elected by the people of the state on the basis of adult franchise and secret ballot.

As election drew near, the Sheikh government tightened its hold over the entire election machinery. As there was no jurisdiction of Indian Election Commission, the National Conference candidates and official machinery intimidated the opposition.[33] However, the Praja Parishad nominated candidates for twenty seven out of thirty electoral constituencies in Jammu region.[34] Forty one out of the forty six nominations filed by the Praja Parishad were rejected on one pretext or the other. In only three constituencies the Praja Parishad's nominations were accepted.[35]

On 22nd September, 1951, the working committee of the Praia Parishad held a meeting and passed a resolution in which they condemned the arbitrary action of the election authorities and gave an ultimatum to the state government to reconsider the rejection of the nomination papers of the Praja Parishad candidates, failing which the Praja Parishad threatened to boycott the election.[36] In a statement issued on 6th October 1951, Pt Prem Nath Dogra, president of the Praja Parishad, blamed the *interim* government of having taken several, arbitrary and unconstitutional measures to pack the assembly with the National Conference.[37] However, no one in the centre government took note of the Praja Parishad's concern. Instead, the centre leaders supported the Sheikh's policies and condemned the Praja Parishad for inciting communalism in the state, which otherwise, they claimed, symbolised the tradition of religious toleration and secularism. Thus, Praja Parishad boycotted the elections and all the National Conference candidates were elected unopposed.

On 31th, October 1951, the state constituent assembly was formed and its first session was held on 5th November 1951. In an attempt to analyse the impact of the assembly's first session and to publicise its points of view on major issues, the Praja Parishad organised a meeting on 11th, November, 1951.[38] In that meeting, the main agenda of the constituent assembly was discussed. Pt Prem Nath Dogra opened that there was no need for a separate state constitution, as we have better the Constitution of India. Praja Parishad viewed that the state's interest lay in complete and unconditional accession. According to them, it was necessary that Indian constitution should be applied to Jammu and Kashmir in the same manner as in other Indian states. Regarding the fate of the royal dynasty, the Parishad condemned the Sheikh and his administration. Pt Prem Nath Dogra rejected the contention of Sheikh Abdullah, that Hari Singh had lost the confidence of all the people of the state. He claimed that except for the National Conference, all the people had full confidence in the Maharaja.[39]

So far as land reforms were concerned, it may be mentioned that Hari Singh was the first Monarch who had given a symbolic expression of land to the tillers when he himself ploughed the land. Consequently, National Conference made it a plank of *Naya Kashmir* and passed the Big *landed Estate Act,* under which land was transferred to the tiller. Pt Prem Nath Dogra insisting in his speech said, "Praja Parishad is not against the transfer of land to the tillers but it favours that proper compensation to the expropriated lords be made in accordance with the Indian constitution".[40]

Praja Parishad Agitation at two Stages, 1952-53

To show its displeasure and anger against the policies of Abdullah's administration, the Praja Parishad organised a campaign to demand total unconditional integration with India. This campaign culminated in a major show down between Praja Parishad and state authorities in early 1952. The situation worsened when on 15th January, 1952, an official function in Government, Gandhi Memorial College in Jammu was organised and in that function National Conference flag was placed along with the Indian flag.[41] About ten to fifteen students of the college staged demonstration against the hoisting of the National Conference flag at the official function within the premises of the college where Sheikh Mohd Abdullah was to speak.

The students complained that the National Conference flag was a party flag and it could not take the place of a national flag.[42] A number of student's leaders were expelled from the college and the state administration came down heavily upon the student's demonstration. Twenty students were arrested and sent to central Jail, Jammu.[43] The students started *satyagrah* and went on fast unto death in the central jail.[44]

To protest against the arrest, a big procession comprising thousands was carried out in the city on 8th February 1952[45]. The procession went to secretariat where they became violent, broke a wall, entered the office, burnt the furniture and office records. Realising the gravity of the situation, the government not only clamped curfew in the city, but sought the help of Indian army to maintain law and order in the city.[46] The distressing reports about Jammu was highlighted by the Indian press. Pt Jawahar Lal Nehru, no doubt, patronised the National Conference and had faith in Sheikh Mohammad Abdullah's secularism, yet he could not face with equanimity the enraged Hindu opinion in India. He advised the state government to defuse the situation by releasing the students and Praja Parishad leaders.[47] On 10th April, 1952, on the advise of central leaders, all the arrested leaders of the Praja Parishad were released as a gesture of goodwill. It was for the first time that the contention of Praja Parishad was recognised by the Congress Government, at Delhi.[48]

Praja Parishad also sent a delegation to New Delhi to submit a petition to the President of India, Dr Rajendra Prasad. In the petition, Praja Parishad claimed the right of the people of Jammu region to determine their own future without interference from National Conference and Sheikh Abdullah administration.[49]

To counter Praja Parishad's contention, the National Conference leaders went as far as to declare that the demand for the integration of the state with Indian union would not be acceptable to the Muslims, who had acceded to India to protect their freedom when Pakistan sought to snatch it. [50]

Sheikh Abdullah, was deeply disturbed by the intensity of the agitation and the articulate support it had received by the Indian press, made a sensational and provocative speech at Ranbir Singhpura.[51] In April, 1952, where he said, "It is very well for the people of India that communalism in India has been finally eliminated but none can deny that communalism spirit still exists in India. Many Kashmere fear, what will happen to them and their position, if for instance something happens to Pandit Nehru. We want to join India without any kind of mental reservation. "He declared, "How can we do so until we are convinced of the complete elimination of communalism in India."[52] He further said that J&K accession to India would have to be of a restricted nature so long as communalism was flourishing on the soil of India. He reminded his audience that the state had acceded to India only in three subjects– defence, foreign affairs and communication.[53] There was no question yet of applying the Indian constitution to Jammu and Kashmir in all respect. He also warned those in India and the state who were in favour of full accession that they would be serving the interest of neither country nor the state and would, in fact, by their very persistence, be destroying the union between the two."[54]

In reaction to the Sheikh's speech the Praja Parishad launched a signature campaign. On 25th June, 1952, they submitted a *memorandum* to the President of India, Dr Rajendra Prashad, signed by five lakh people in which people of Jammu claimed the right to determine their own future and wanted the entire constitution of India to apply to Jammu.[55] The movement launched by Praja Parishad not only received a wide coverage in the Indian press, but some Congressmen also started paying attention to the Jammu problem.

Delhi Agreement

In the face of growing crises, the Indian government summoned Sheikh Abdullah to New Delhi for consultations. The consultation outcome of the discussion was an understanding popularly known as "Delhi Agreement."[56] The terms were revealed by Indian Prime Ministry on the floor of Indian Parliament on July 24th,1952. The Jammu and Kashmir constituent assembly discussed this agreement and finally adopted a motion on 21st August, 1952. The agreement was discussed in the Union parliament on 25th August, 1952, and was accepted.[57]

In this agreement, it was agreed that the hereditary ruler Maharaja Hari Singh would be replaced by an elected head of the state, while the flag of India was to be recognised as supreme but the state was allowed to have its own flag. The jurisdiction of the Indian Supreme Court was limited. All residuary powers were vested in the state and the emergency powers of the Indian President within the state was curtailed. On its part, the state government agreed to examine the need for fundamental rights in the new constitution and the desirability of some degree of economic integration with India.[58]

Delhi Agreement caused grave apprehensions among the Hindus and other minorities. People in Jammu felt restive. However, ignoring the Praja Parshid's demands by Sheikh Abdullah on 12th November, 1952 formally adopted an amendment to the constitution replacing the Maharaja by that of an elected Head of state "Sadar-i-Riyst"[59]

On 23rd October, 1952, Pt Prem Nath Dogra, president of Praja Parishad held a press conference in New Delhi and declared Praja Parishad will start a satyagrah in Jammu. His initiative was supported by the other parties like Jan Sangh and Hindu Maha Sabha. [60]

On 18th November, 1952, Praja Parishad held a meeting in which they decided to launch a movement against the decision of the state government and a number of resolutions were passed, demanding deletion of Article 370 from the constitution and full integration of state with India.[61]

The state government adopting brutal methods to suppress the movement and opened fired on demonstrators gathering at Ranbir Singhpura, Sunderbani, Akhnoor, Samba and Kishtwar. Consequently, 30 persons were killed, 131 wounded and 1,300 sent in jails custody. Twenty women had also took a remarkable part in the struggle.[62] This movement assumed serious proportions and its repercussions were felt outside the state also.[63] A Hindu volunteer carried a Indian national flag in his hands, and removing the red National Conference flag which was hoisted on the top of the official building, hoisted the tricolour in its place.[64]

Meanwhile, the armed police came, fired tear gas at the procession to disperse and shoot at the volunteers and warn them to desist from doing what every Indian was doing as a patriotic citizen. The movement assumed serious proportion and its echo was felt outside the state also. Its case was taken up by like minded parties at Delhi. Dr Shyama Prasad Mukasjee and W.C. Chatterji decided to launch a satyagrah as on all India basis.[65]

The brutal behaviour of the government was condemned by Dogra Sabha, the oldest social organisation of the state.[66] During January and February of 1953, Mr Shyama Prasad Mukharji the then President of the Jan Sangh entered into an animated correspondence with Pt Jawahar Lal Nehru and Sheikh Mohammad Abdullah on the problem of Jammu. It was Mukesjee's view that the agitation grew out of fear and doubts among the Jammu people about the future of the state under Sheikh Mohammad Abdullah.[67] He criticised Sheikh Mohammad Abdullah for having treated the people of Jammu region as second class citizen. On 13th

February, 1953, he wrote to Sheikh Abdullah, "India has been torn into two by the two nation theory. You are now developing a three nation theory, the third being the Kashmir nation"[68]

Similarly, the Akali leaders Master Tara Singh also extended fullest support to the Praja Parishad movement.[69] Whereas public voice in India became more and more critical of the doing of the National Conference government.[70] However in 1953, at Hyderabad session, Nehru in a conference publicly said, the Jammu people suffered from certain economic hardship. This statement of Nehru not only confirmed the apprehension of the Jammuites but authenticated a partial success of the Praja Parishad movement.[71]

On 5th April, 1953, when Sheikh Mohammad Abdullah was on his way to Srinagar near Banihal he said, "If Jammu people cannot live with us, they are free to go their own way we will go our own. Good bye to Jammu". This attitude of Sheikh Mohd. Abdullah was not only criticised by Congressmen at the session of Indian National Congress but he was hooted at Delhi while addressing audiences. As a result, Sheikh Abdullah decided to make some concessions to the people of Jammu and Laddakh.[73]

A constitution was prepared on the basis of federal principles.[74] It divided the state into five units each with an autonomous administration.[75] The area on the other side of the ceasefire had also taken into account for this purpose. The plan envisaged the present territory of the state to be divided into three autonomous provinces, Kashmir, Jammu and Laddakh.[76] The Dogra and the Buddhist rejected this plan because the real executive power was to be retained by Muslims of Kashmir who were in majority.[77] Pt Prem Nath Dogra of Jammu and *Kushok Bakula* (Head of Lama of sprituk Monastery) of Laddakh declared any attempt to implement the plan would lead to the complete separation of Jammu and Laddakh from the state. [78]

With the failure of the Mukerjee-Nehru negotiations over the settlement of Jammu dispute, in March 1953, the three Hindu parties in India *Jan Sangh, The Maha Sabha, The Ram Rajya decided to* start a joint *satyagraha* in Delhi in support to the Praja Parishad's demands.[79] These parties organised a demonstration, protests and courted arrests in major towns and cities in India. The arrest of people and lathi-charge on processions became a routine. Nearly 4,000 people were imprisoned. The intensity of Jammu campaign was undoubtedly heightened by the forces outside the state in which[80], the neighbouring Punjab also was effected, the same type of brutal lathi-charge and tear-gas was resorted[81] consequently. Hundreds of non-violent *satyagrahi* were injured.[82]

In Kashmir, *Kushok Bakula*, the undisputed leader of Laddakh, declared his support for full integration of Kashmir with Bharat (India). He warned in case steps were not taken to do so, there was a danger for Laddakh going over the Tibet.[83]

Visit of Mukherjee

Certain prominent Hindu leaders of India desired to tour the Jammu region to ascertain the real conditions of life and the views of the people.[84]

In an effort to cut off the influx of agitators from outside of the state, the Sheikh Abdullah's administration issued an ordinance banning the entry of any person into state without a permit. This action spurred Dr Shyama Prashad Mukerjee, the leader of Jan Sangh to challenge the ordinance. On 11th May, 1953, Dr Shyam Prashad Mukerjee, with his associates entered the state without any permission.[85] The Indian government allowed them to go but they were arrested by the state police while on his way to Jammu.[86] The news about his arrest spread all over the state. To protest against his arrest, a complete *hartal* was observed in Jammu province. During *hartal* protest processions were taken out.[87] The result was that all this created political instability, suspense, uncertainty and economic stress.[88]

Meanwhile, the custodial death of Dr Shyama Prashad Mukerjee on 23rd June" 1953 in detentions at Srinagar the whole North of India plunged in profound grief and became anti-Nehru and anti-Abdullah[89]. Sheikh Mohammad Abdullah wrote, when Dr Mukerjee was in prison, Pt Jawahar Lal Nehru and Maulana Azad visited Kashmir but neither of them both bothered to meet him. But when I got information about his sickness in solitary confinement I ordered that Pt Prem Nath Dogra who was arrested in Jammu in connection with the agitation of the Praja Parishad should be one day brought to Srinagar and lodged with Dr Mukerjee. I was informed by Pt Sham Lal, Minister of Jails, that Dr Mukejee has suffered a massive heart attack. I was shocked.[90]

Praja Parishad refused to believe the death occurred in natural circumstances. Jammu region was furious over his death, because he gave his life for their cause of the nation.[91] On 3rd July, 1953, Sheikh Abdullah declared that he would visit New Delhi to discuss the internal crises in the state. Both Bakshi Gulam Mohammad, who was the Minister of Law and Deputy Prime Minister, Mirza Afzal Beg, the Revenue Minister travelled to the Indian capital "New Delhi". Pt Prem Nath Dogra, Praja Parishad president, who had been released immediately after Mukerjee's death, was also present in New Delhi during this time.[92] Within a few days, Prime Minister, J.L. Nehru, returned from London and found country in grief. It was because of his efforts the two rival groups evolved a truce.[93] The Praja Parishad agitation was called off on 7th July, 1953, both in Jammu as well as in Delhi. The state government agreed to release all political prisoners and to take positive steps to implement their role of the Delhi Agreement.[94]

However, Sheikh Abdullah was opposed to any further concession involving the state relationship with the Indian union.[95] He refused to approve any step that would bind the state more closely to the centre Government.[96] Simultaneously, there were inflammatory reports that Sheikh Abdullah was thinking of declaring Kashmir independent. An open rift in the National Conference suddenly developed which led to Sheikh Abdullah's ministry towards end. There were a number of causes which were responsible for the dismissal of Abdullah's ministry. These were Praja Parishad agitation, opposition within the party, sharp differences of opinion among the members of the working committee of National Conference which soon brought state cabinet within its orbit. Bakshi Gulam Mohammad adhered to the view the Kashmir should continue to remain with India but Sheikh Abdullah was against it and criticised the state accession with India. When Pt Nehru invited Sheikh Abdullah for further talks, Sheikh Abdullah refused to come.[97]

Pt Saraf, Bakshi Gulam Mohammad and Girdhari Lal Dogra informed the Sadar-i-Riyst, Karan Singh, that there is division in cabinet and Sheikh Mohammad Abdullah had lost majority of votes in the cabinet, so he should be dismissed.[98] Sheikh Abdullah contradicted their claim. But Sadar-i-Riyst, Karan Singh, on his own sources dismissed Sheikh Mohd Abdullah from Ministership on 8th August, 1953; Sheikh Abdullah was arrested.[99] On 9th August, 1953, Bakshi Gulam Mohammad was invited by Sadar-i-Riyst, Karan Singh, to form a new government.[100]

The transfer of power from Jammu to the hands of Kashmere leadership an apprehension emerge in Jammu region that the Muslim leaders of National Conference would follow an anti-Dogra policies; the enactment of Big Landed Estate Abolition Act., strengthened their apprehension. Special status under Article 370 of the Indian constitution gave a concern to Jammuities to protest against the Government to have full integration with Indian constitution.

References

1. Sharma, S.C., *Partition: Pak Invasion of 1947–A Study of Socio-economic Consequences*, p. 5.
2. *Ibid.*
3. General Department, *Chief Secretariat, Emergency Admmistration Order No. 176-H of 1947*, 30th October, 1947.
4. *Ibid.*
5. *Ibid.*
6. Bazaz, P.N., op. cit., p. 565.
7. Teng, M.K. and Koul, R.K., op. cit., Pp. 493-495.
8. Singh Karan (op. cit. pp. 123) *Hair Apparent: An Autobiography,* Delhi, Oxford University Press., 1982, p. 132.
9. *Ibid.*
10. Puri Balraj, op. cit., pp. 18-23.
11. Modhak Balraj, *Kashmir Centre of New Alignments*, Deepak Prakashan, New Delhi, 1987, pp. 37-111.
12. Bimonthly, *Kashmir Affairs,* Delhi, No. 3, January-February, 1950, p. 10.
13. *Ibid*.
14. *Ibid*, and Singh, Karan; *Hair Apparent: An Autobiography,* Delhi Oxford University Press, 1982, p. 132.
15. Singh, Karan, op. cit., p. 133.
16. Puri, Balraj, p. 38.
17. Verma, Durga Dass, *Constitution of J & K, Praja Parishad Article* (Iqbal Press, Jammu) p. 2.
18. *Kashmir Problem and Jammu Satyagraha-An Objective Study*, Bharatiya Jan Sangh, Delhi, N.P., p. 25.
19. *Ibid.*
20. Bamzai, P.N.K., op. cit., p. 806.
21. *Ranbir*, Jammu, March 15th and 6th, 1949. p. 7.

22. *Ibid.*
23. *Ibid.*
24. *Such*, Jammu, February 7th,1950, p. 11.
25. Teng, M.K., op. cit., pp. 63-64.
26. Anand, A.S., op. cit., p. 128.
27. *Ibid*, op. cit, pp. 130-131.
28. Teng, M.K., op. cit., p. 66.
29. *The Chand*, Jammu, 12th November, 1950, p. 14.
30. *Desh Sewak*, Weekly, Jammu, 20th November, 1951.
31. Saraf, Mulak Raj, op cit., p. 54.
32. Teng, M.K., op. cit., p. 66.
33. *Ibid.*
34. *Ibid*, op. cit., p. 67.
35. *Ibid.*
36. *Ibid.*
37. *Tribune*, Ambala, January 15th, 1952, p. 9.
38. Mahdak, Balraj, op cit., p. 57.
39. David, Lockwood, op cit., p. 174.
40. *Hindustan Times*, June 25th, 1952, p. 9.
41. *Ibid.*
42. *Ibid.*
43. *Ibid.*
44. Bimonthly, *Kashmir Affairs*, Delhi, No.7, March-April 1952, p. 21.
45. Edison, David, op. cit., p. 77.
46. Puri, Balraj, op cit., p. 98.
47. Baziz, P.N. op. cit., p. 570.
48. *Ibid*.
49. *Hindustan Times*, June 25th, 1952, p. 10.
50. *Ranbir*, Jammu, 10th July, 1952.
51. Saraf M.R., op cit., p. 143 and *Jammu Situation; Nehru-Mukerjee - Abdullah correspondence*, January-February 1953, Canton Press, New Delhi, p. 39.

52. Gupta, Sisler, *Kashmir - A study In India-Pakistan Relations*, 1966, p. 143.
53. Bushan, Vidhya, op. cit., p. 180.
54. *Ibid.*
55. Verma, Durga Dass, *Constitution of J & K*, Praja Parishad, Article, Iqbal Press, Jammu, p. 2.
56. *Hindustan Standard*, New Delhi, February, 10th, 1953.
57. Anand, AS., op. cit., Pp. 152 - 153.
58. *Ibid.*
59. *An Objective Study*, Bhartiya Jan Singh, Delhi, (ND), p. 734.
60. *Hind Samachar*, Jullundur, December, 25th, 1952, p. 14. *Ibid.*
61. *Ibid.*
62. *Ibid.*
63. *Ibid.*
64. Bazaz, P.N., op. cit., p. 579.
65. *Ibid.*
66. *Desh Sewak*, Weekly, Jammu, March 14th, 1953.
67. *Documents: Mukerjee, Nehru, Abdullah correspondence*, pp. 37-102.
68. *Ibid.*
69. Lockwood, David, op. cit., p. 193.
70. Dhar, Triloknath, *History of Kashmir - A Peep into the Past, Kashmir Samachar, Political Article in Kashmir, www.Kashmir information. com/Kashmiri/Kashmer Affairs, Ltd.*
71. Bazaz, P.N., op. cit., p. 583.
72. Bimonthly, *Kashmir Affairs*, Delhi No. 15th, May, 1953, p. 7.
73. *Ibid.*
74. Saraf, M.R., op. cit., p. 144
75. Bakshi, S.R., op. cit., p. 88

76. Korbll, Joecph, op. cit., p. 2-4.
77. Bakshi, S. R., op. cit., p. 88.
78. *Ibid.*
79. *The Tribune*, Ambala. 15th May, 1953. p. 10.
80. *Ibid.*
81. *Ibid.*
82. Vidhya Bhushan, op. cit., p. 184.
83. *Facing Internal Threats of Nations Integrity, HAP/ WWW. Hindu books.org/vision/ch.2html.*, p. 5.
84. *Ibid.*
85. *Ibid.*
86. *Ibid.*
87. Jackwood, David, op. cit., p. 209.
88. *Kashmir Times*, Jammu, 25th June, 1953, p. 7.
89. Bazaz, P.N., op. cit., p. 589.
90. Bhushan, Vidhya, op. cit., p. 187.
91. *Ibid.*
92. *Ibid.*
93. Lockwoo, David, op. cit., p. 218.
94. Puri, Balraj, p. 116.
95. *Ibid*.
96. Bose, Sumantra, *The Challenge in Kashmir, Democracy, Self-determination and a Just Peace*, Sage Publication, New Delhi, 1997, p. 32.
97. Bazaz, P.N., op. cit., p. 665.
98. Qasim, Mir, op. cit., p. 67.
99. *Documents on Jammu and Kashmir*: Sadar-i-Riyst's letter to Sheikh Abdullah Srinagar, 8th August, 1953, p. 23 and order issued by the Sadar-i-Riyst on 8th August, 1953, Srinagar, p. 24.
100. *Documents on Jammu and Kashmir:* Sadar-i-Riyst's letter to Bakshi Gulam Mohammad, 9th August, 1953, Srinagar.

6

DISCONTENT OVER THE DISPARITIES, 1957-1967

After 1947, political power was transferred from the hands of Dogra rulers to Kashmere leadership. The new leadership raised the bogey of deprivation during Maharaja's rule and it lay its root deep in Jammu region. As discussed in last chapter, that Jammu[1] was passing through a series of nerve-shattering incidents because of anti-Jammu stance of Kashmere leaders.[2]

The Jammu region, an important part of the state of Jammu and Kashmir, had been ignored so far. It was generally felt that Government favoured the valley at the expense of Jammu's interests, needs and aspirations. Hence, Jammu region has constantly been engaged in assertion or its own "distinct identity". The distinct identity of Jammu region got itself articulated in the form of various demands. In this process, the Praja Parishad and RSS became more articulate in rising their voice against the anti-Jammu policy of the state government. In addition, they were in favour of complete integration of Jammu and Kashmir state with Indian union and abrogation of Article 370 of Indian constitution.[3]

After the arrest of Sheikh Mohammad Abdullah on 9th Augusta, 1937, there arose tension between Kashmir and the rest of India. The Praja Parishad leaders, RSS and Balraj

Puri highlighted explosive potentialities of Jammu problem. They repeatedly pleaded for autonomy of the state within India and Jammu within the state, so that aspirations of Jammu as well as of the Kashmir were equally satisfied. But it was unfortunate that in the name of national interest or the interest of the nation, the awakening in Jammu had been silenced off and on.[4]

The wide spread of dissatisfaction and feeling among the people of Jammu was because that they were being discriminated, neglected, and political importance was given to Kashmir only.[5] It was also noted that Jammu people from Jammu region got employed in the rest of India. So, social, economic, cultural, religious, caste division and uneven developments of Jammu region were largely responsible for intra-regional tension.[6]

Jammu has expressed its discontent many a times and through many ways. It was noted that Jammu's discontent was because of economic and administrative policies, disparities and not getting proper share in political power. Jammu was ruled by the Kashmir government which was were not interested to deal with the Jammu people and wanted to rule without sharing problems with its people.[7]

The policy of victimising Jammu in the name of Kashmir and exploiting Kashmir in the name of *Kashmeriat* led to a tendency which cut at the very root of the state's integrity. This resulted in the widening of gulf between Jammu and Kashmir and thus, giving a free hand to political exploiters. In order to safeguard Jammu's interest, Jammuites were demanding from Kashmir, what the Kashmeres were asking from New Delhi, i.e., internal autonomy. However, after assuming the reign of the state government, Bakshi Gulam Mohammad tried to accommodate popular local leadership to a responsible limit because the political and economic situation. Kashmir in the early months of

1953 was passing through crisis.[9] The people in general and National Conference in particular was astounded at the change of attitude of Sheikh Abdullah towards the position of the state to the Indian union. The majority of the working committee's members headed by Bakshi Gulam Mohammed were opposed to the attitude adopted by Sheikh.[10]

An open rift developed in the cabinet because Sheikh Abdullah moved against his detractors in the cabinet, and asked for the resignation of his Health Minister, Pt Sham Lal Saraf. Pt Sham Lal Saraf refused to resign unless the whole cabinet was dissolved and a new government was formed. On 8th August, a joint memorandum signed by BK Ghulam Mohammad, Finance Minister G.L. Dogra and Pt. Sham Lal Saraf, accusing Sheikh Abdullah was submitted to the Sadar-i-Riyst, accusing him trying to precipitate a rupture in the relationship of the state with India and informing the Prime Minister that in their view the cabinet had lost the confidence of the people. The memorandum informed that the Sheikh Abdullah had lost the confidence of the people in the cabinet, whereas the economic distress of the people has considerably increased which needs prompt and serious attention. In the memorandum, they also mentioned that honest and efficient administration has become impracticable in the state.[11]

An emergency meeting of the cabinet was held on 8th August, 1953 under the presidentship of Sadar-i-Riyst. The Sadar-i-Riyst fearing a great threat to the unity and integrity in the state, acted promptly with the support of the centrel government and issued an order on 8th August, 1953; he said, "I, Karan Singh, Sadar-i-Riyst, functioning in the interest of the people of the state, who have reposed the responsibility and authority of the hardship of the state in me, do hereby dismiss Sheikh

Mohammad Abdullah from the Prime-Ministership of the state of Jammu and Kashmir and consequently the council of Ministers headed by him is dissolved forth with." [12]

On 9th August, 1953, Sadar-i-Riyst issued an order and invited Bakshi Gulam Mohmmad to form a new government and adviced him to constitute immediately a new cabinet so as to avoid political and administrative vacuum. He also made it clear that the continuance in office of the new cabinet will depend upon its securing a vote of confidence from the legislative assembly during its coming session.[13]

On 9th August, 1953, Bakshi Ghulam Mohammad took the oath in office. In his broadcast to the state people, he said, "It had been a painful decision for them to part from their erstwhile colleagues, but in times of historic crises, when the fate of millions was at stake, personal relations and affections had to be subordinated to the paramount interest of the country". "An independent Kashmir continued Bakshi Gulam Mohammed, "under the influence of an imperialist power will be a grave threat to freedom and independence of India and Pakistan"[14]

The new cabinet, consisted of Bakshi Gulam Mohammad, G.M. Sadiq, Mr Qasim, Sham Lal Saraf and Girdhari Lal Dogra, was formed. Bakshi devised a number of schemes to bring about all-round development and to clear the mess that the Sheikh's dispensation had created[15]. The state constituent assembly had confirmed the accession to India and agreed on a constitution which had come into effect on 26th January, 1957. This brought the state at par with other Indian states in respect of financial matters including proportionate allocation of funds from the centre. [16] The state entered into financial arrangement with union government in 1957.

However, Sheikh's supporters led by Afzal Beg under the banner of plebiscite made a one-point programme that "Democracy had been murdered on 9th August, 1953, with Sheikh's arrest, the constituent assembly was no longer representative of the people's will and, therefore, all its decisions were null and void". It is based on this theory, that the National Conference time and again raised the bogey of pre-1953.

The popular government, after coming in power not only abolished the *Jagirdaris* system but old concept of martial races came to an end, which deprived the Rajputs of this region from their land and privileged position in the state army and police. Similarly, the *Jagmani* system disintegrated. Obviously, every segment of the society had to look for new avenues for their livelihood, which could be possible only after getting proper education and training in new skills.[17]

To meet this requirement in 1958-59, an Industrial Training Institute was established in Jammu. In 1960-61, a Polytechnic College was opened at Jammu, where the students were provided training in three years diploma course in Civil, Electrical, Mechanical and Auto-Mobile Engineering. In addition, this institute also provides two years Draftsman course. [18]

For professions like medicine and engineering, it was only in 1959-60 that a Medical *and a* Regional Engineering College was established in Srinagar. In Jammu, only an Ayurvedic College was opened In 1961, To impart education in agriculture, there was no agriculture college in the state till 1960, but soon after two agricultural colleges were opened, one at R.S. Pura in Jammu and the other at Sopore in Kashmir. [19]

Despite these developments, there was a growing demand among the people of the Jammu region that separate medical and *engineering* colleges should be opened in Jammu. But in the meantime, the state government closed down the Agriculture College at R.S. Pura in 1967. The same year, admission to the Ayurvedic

College was brought down from 25 to 10 students, rather a first step towards its closure which ultimately come in 1976.[20]

Similarly, the people of Jammu region got less representation in government employment, which made them conscious of the fact that this deprivation was because of the transfer of power from Jammu to Kashmir leadership. The problem aggravated with the publication of 1961 census report. According to which, Jammu's population was 16 lakhs and that of Kashmir 18 lakhs. But Kashmir hade 12 additional seats in state assembly, similarly in Lok Sabha, Jammu was given two seats as against three in Kashmir. But what Bakshi Ghulam Mohd did was altogether contrary to the expectation of the people of Jammu. Political power, decision making, administration at higher levels, better deal in matters relating to employment, the location of prestigious institution and funds for development became a privilege of Kashmir alone. Total centralisation of the state apparatus in Bakshi's hand allowed enormous scope for corruption, as a substantial portion of the centre's financial aid was misappropriated by the top layer of the ruling elite. His regime was nick named as Bakshi Brothers Corporation. Kashmir as given the right to have 12 additional seats.

Obviously feeling the absence of freedom under Bakshi, G.M. Sadiq and D.P. Dhar had launched the Democratic National Conference. However, his regime continued till October 1963, when he was dropped under the Kamraj Plan. He was succeeded by Mr Shams-ud-Din. On assuming the charge of Prime Ministership, he announced that he would follow the footsteps of BK Ghulam Mohammad. This sent a wave of resentment in Jammu. The Praja Parishad organised a protest and demonstration in Jammu on the opening of *Durbar* in winter capital of the state. Hundred persons were injured on either side. The demand of the Praja Parishad was President's rule, abolition of Article 370 of the Indian constitution and opened enquiry into corruption charges against ministers. [21]

Meanwhile, the holy relic enshrined at the Hazartbal Mosque was stolen in December, 1963. The news caused widespread dismay and anger among the people. This event has, however, revealed the short- comings of the Shams-ud-Din ministry. With the active help and efforts of the centrel government, the holy relic was restored at the shrine. However, the National Conference legislators elected Mr G.M. Sadiq as the new leader who assumed the office of Prime Minister in February 1964. [22]

Ghulam Mohd Sadiq, the new incumbent, filled the hearts of the people with a new hope. His appointment as the Prime Minister of the state was taken by the people to mean the beginning of a new era, full of hope and promise for the future. Ghulam Mohd Sadiq, who is still remembered and hailed by all section 'of the people' profession, different political ideologies as a true democrat, professional and secular, approved instrumental in bringing about historic changes leading of the Kashmeres, unification with India. The National Conference was dissolved and got merged with the Indian National Congress in 1965. At about the same time, the office of Sadar-i-Riyst and that of the Prime Minister were substituted by those of the Governor and Chief Minister respectively. [23]

G.M. Sadiq adopted conciliatory policy towards Sheikh and his associates. On 5th April, acting on Nehru's instructions bypassing the Home Ministry in Delhi, the Prime Minister of Kashmir, G.M. Sadiq, announced that the case against Sheikh Abdullah was being withdrawn immediately. The Sheikh was released on 8th April.[24] However, no radical departure in the government's approach was made towards Jammu. The Jammu

Autonomy Forum formed in 1966 demanded internal Political autonomy. Ideologically close to the Indian socialist movement, the Forum was supported by the Jammu and Kashmir Youth Conference and Friends of New Kashmir at New Delhi. It urged appreciation of the secular character to Jammu's political demand and need for constitutional and institutional arrangements of power sharing. The Forum sought democratisation of the state's political structure, a neutral civil administration distinct from the National Conference organisation, and economic amelioration through a planned economic policy. The Jammu Autonomy Forum presented a memorandum to the state and centrel government and articulated its demands through press and platform. Supported by a small segment of Jammu's intelligentsia, it failed to mobilise mass support. The idea of regional autonomy provoked stiff opposition from the entire political spectrum. The Jan Sangh (Praja parishad had merged in Jan Sangh) charged that it would benefit only the supporters of Shaikh Abdullah and pro-Pakistan elements. The Plebiscite Front debunked it as a game of Indian imperialism. The Congress denounced the disruptionist slogan as being against national interests and alongwith the Jan Sangh attributed the idea to a foreign hand. An Ekta Front was setup to co-ordinate the anti-autonomy campaign. According to *Hindustan Times, "The strength of the move of autonomy is advocated not so much by what its protagonists have been able to achieve so far as by the amount of resistance it has aroused".* Diverse elements have combined to oppose it tooth and nail. The controversy only served the Forum's objective in projecting regional autonomy as an alternative solution to Jammu's grievances.[25]

Merger of Jammu with Himachal Pradesh

The formula of then Sadar-i-Riyst, Dr Karan Singh of trifurcating the state along linguistic lines – Jammu to

Jamum to merged into Himachal Pradesh, Ladakha to be a centrally administrated area and Kashmir valley a separate unlingual state, aroused similar reactions. [26]

It was severely criticised by the communists on the left, who believed, it was part of some sinister, American plot, Jan Sangh considered that by isolating Kashmir, the Muslim would be so preponderant that we would lose it to Pakistan. The state government debunked both proposals and used its resources to crush the demand for regional autonomy. Sadiq denounced Karan Singh's formula as an important idea which was fought with dangerous consequences and should be resisted with 'all overnight.' [27]

In 1966, the state government closed down the agriculture college in R.S. Pura and reduced the intake strength of students in Ayurvedic College from 25 to 10. As Jammu was already resisting against regional imbalances, thus further aggravated the situation. There was a student unrest in Jammu, during which four students, namely, Brij Mohan, Gurcharan Singh, Subash Chander, Gulshan Handa were killed and 50 others were injured in police-firing on 17th October, 1966.[28] The other people injured in police firing on 17th October, 1966 were Kamal Sharma (J & K Students Congress president), Raj Thakur, Varinder Dev, S. Sawarn Singh, etc.

It shook the faith of Jammuites in the state administration and its leadership. In this process in 1967, Dogra Mandal, the Jammu Autonomy Forum and Student's Congress came in to being. All these organisations not only gave vent to their anguish over the atrocious acts of the police but they felt discrimination in every sphere, i.e., development, employment and education.[29]

They demanded the establishment of Regional Development Boards, Regional Recruitment Board, Separate University for Jammu, as well as Medical College.[30]

The state government in consultation with the Union Government on November 6th, 1967, appointed a three member Commission of Inquiry, under the Chairmanship of P. B. Gajender Gadkar, Retired Chief Justice of India. Two other members of the commission were Shanker Prasad (New Delhi) and Badr-ud-din Tyabji (Hyderabad), whereas B.D. Bagchi was appointed a secretary to the Commission (IAS).

The term of reference to the Commission were:

(a) To make assessment of the development programmes opportuned to the various regions of the state and to recommend measures necessary to give assurance that the resources available to the state govemment are being shared equitably and also to convey a feeling of equal participation in the integrated development of the state.

(b) To examine the recruitment policies of government and to recommend measures for giving an equitable share in government employment to the various regions and communities, having special regard to the claim of the scheduled castes and other economically, educationally and socially backward communities, classes and groups among the citizens of the state consistently with the maintenance of efficiency of administration.

(c) To examine the policies of the state government regarding admission to institutions of higher education and the scheme of assistance by way of scholarships and the loans, with a view to ensuring an equitable distribution of the available facilities to the various regions and communities, having special regard to the claims of the Scheduled Castes and other economically, educationally and socially backward communities, classes and groups among the citizens of the state.

(d) To acquaint itself of the ground situation, the commission visited the three regions of the state taking memoranda and representations embodying details on the problems, local or otherwise the people faced.

After the arrest of SM Abdullah on 9th August, 1953, and formation of new Government by Bakshi Gulam Mohammad, the people of Jammu began resisting the discrimination which they were being subjected on two crucial matters, i.e., economic and administrative policies. They demanded the establishment of the Regional Development Boards, Regional Recruitment Boards, separate university for Jammu and medical as well as engineering college for Jammu region as it was in Kashmir. The result was the establishment of enquiry commission in November 1967 known as Gajendra Gadkar Commission.

Note References

1. Mahajan, Hari Om, *Beyond the Kashmir Valley,* p. 169.
2. Puri, Balraj, *Jammu - A clue to Kashmir Tangle,* pp. 18-24.
3. Koul, Sham Lai, Kachhru, Om Kar Nath, *Jammu, Kashmir, Laddakh–Ringside View,* p. 324, Atlantic Publishers, New Delhi, 1999.
4. Puri Balraj, p. 31.
5. *Ibid.*, p. 53.
6. Koul, Sham Lal, Kachhru, Omkar Nath, p. 324.
7. "Explosive Potentialities of Jammu Problem", Bimonthly *Kashmir Affairs,* Article, Delhi, No. 11, May-June, 1961, p. 5.
8. Regional Tension, *Economic and Political Weekly,* 2nd February, 1967, p. 3.
9. *Ibid.*
10. *Kashmir Times,* Jammu, January, 1966, p. 3.
11. A joint *Memorandum* submitted by Cabinet Members of the Sheikh Mohammad Ahdullah's Ministry to the Sadar-i-Riyst, 8th August, 1953, pp. 1-45, Srinagar Archive.
12. *Sadar-i-Riyst's Letter to Sheikh Mohammad Abdullah,* Karan Mahal, Srinagar, August 8th, 1953, pp. 1-50.
13. *Order* issued by the Sadar-i-Riyst on 8th August, 1953, Srinagar p. 3.
14. *Bakshi Gulam Mohammad's reply to Sadar-i-Riyst,* Srinagar, 9th August, 1953, Srinagar Archive.
15. *Order* Issued by the Sadar-i-Riyst on 8th August, Srinagar Archive, p. 7.
16. Bamzai, P.N.K., p. 813.
17. Sharma, S.C., *Development of Education in Jammu Region,* p. 1-23
18. *Ibid.* p. 24
19. *Ibid.*
20. *Ibid.*
21. Bamzai, P.N.K., p. 818.
22. "Explosive Potentialities of Jammu problem", *Kashmir Affairs,* March-April, 1964, Srinagar, p. 2.
23. *Ibid.*
24. Karan Singh Formula, *Janata,* 16th January, 1966, Jammu, p. 5.

25. Three units in search of common identity, *Statesman*, 5-6th April, 1966, pp. 3-7.
26. Singh, Karan, p. 29.
27. Puri, Bairaj, *Simmering Volcano: A Study of Jammu Relation with Kashmir,* Sterling, New Delhi, 1983, p. 42.
28. *Ibid.s*
29. Jag Mohan, *My Frozen Turbulence,* Allied Publishers, New Delhi, 1991, p. 219.
30. *Kashmir Times,* Pp. 1-2, 18th October, 1967.

7

JAMMU DEMOCRATIC TURMOIL, 1967-1977

The political power of Jammu region was, in fact, mainly determined in reaction to the politics of Kashmir because demands and aspirations of Jammu region were more or less articulated as a response to the demands and aspirations of Kashmir.[1]

The Jammu region an important ingredient of the state had been ignored so far. The problem of Jammu region in its present context is not only regional identity but of "Regional identity along with Regional unity".[2] *A* feeling of regional discrimination and absence of share in political power, too, become the determinant features of the post-independence politics of Jammu region with the intention of popular rule in the state. The National Conference dominated the political scene of Jammu and Kashmir[3].

In response to the nature of politics in Kashmir as well as a feeling of political deprivation, the Jammu politics, since independence has revolved mainly around two issues – first the greater integration of the state with rest of India and secondly a great role for the Jammu region within the framework of the state politics. The first demand relating to the abrogation of Article 370 required a constitutional amendment, while the later demand revolved around the questions of regional autonomy.[4]

The group, which was mainly responsible for spearheading the idea of Jammu's identity and regional autonomy, was the Jammu Autonomy Forum. The Forum highlighted the problems of tension and irritations in three regions of the state and consistently continued to project the cause of Jammu region throughout sixties and seventies. According to Balraj Puri, "The lack of adequate share in political power is the most important irritant of Jammu region. According to him, "On getting its share in political power Jammu region's poverty might become less bearable. But without power and freedom even prosperity can not keep it happy".[5]

The leaders of the Autonomy Forum stressed the need for reorganisation of the structural pattern of the state of Jammu and Kashmir and giving it a federal shape. The Forum believed that the distinct identity of the three regions of the state Jammu, Kashmir and Laddakh makes it imperative for such a structural reorganisation, whereas the *Kashmeriat,* the identity of Kashmir, needs to be zealously watched and the identity of Laddakh as well as Jammu also needs to be protected. [6]

It was urged by the supporters of regional autonomy that a policy of victimising Jammu on the name of Kashmir was suppressing Kashmir with the fear of Jammu, leads to a tendency which cuts of the every root of the state integrity resulting in the widening of gulf between Jammu and Kashmir and thus creating wide scope for exploiters. [7]

It was argued by the leaders of Autonomy Forum that Jammu with a population of 44 per cent of whole state, was represented by not more than 16 per cent of Secretariat staff and less in many others departments. According to the 1961 Census, the state has an area of about 139,000 square kilometere'. The state constitutes more than two-thirds of the area but has less than two and a half per cent of the population.[8]

It also further urged that disparity lay between the sections within each community. Thus, Hindus population of the state, had hardly one-third of the share. In the administration likewise, the share of six lakh Muslims of Jammu out of the so called Muslims quota was too negligible. Jobs were given on political grounds and genuine interest of community as of regions was being ignored[9].

The Autonomy Forum favoured for reorganisation of the state on the basis of equality and friendship among three regions.[10] The issue raised by the Autonomy Forum and demands raised by them in memorandum were concretised, which was pointed to go into the question of discrimination against Jammu region. In its memorandum they suggested, while a number of subjects proposed to be deleted to the hill area of Assam should broadly form the basis of a similar division in case of Jammu and Kashmir state. The regional administration may broadly follow the pattern of Metropolitan council with which Parliament shares some of its legislature and executive power over the union territory. It is also argued, that a part of the power that the state enjoys within the Indian union should be transferred to its three regions, Jammu, Kashmir and Laddakh.[11]

The quest for Jammu's identity in response to Kashmir's domination over political power had taken another shape. The question of Jammu's identity was raised by different political groups and different organisations during 50s and 60s. RSS, Praja Parishad and Jan Sangh (BJP) were the major forces which dealt with the problem of Jammu region and stressed the need to abolish Article 370, so as to provide both justice to Jammu as well as to Kashmir. The RSS had been most organised socio-political group which had substantial influence on Hindu dominated area of Jammu region.

This had been the first organisation to raise the demand for abrogation of Article 370.[12]

Another major political organisation which took up a stand and voiced its concern against the Kashmir domination was the Praja Parishad.[13] In 1964, it was merged with the Jan Sangh and became the symbolic of the Hindu Nationalism in the state. The Chief Minister, Bakshi Ghulam Mohammad, had not done much for Jammu region, during his long hold over the power with in the state. A feeling started developing that in political, social and economic development, Jammu was being discriminated against.[14]

The Gajendra Gadkar Commission received 93 memoranda from various political, social and religious sections and communities of the society (see Appendix).[15] A little over one-third were from the valley, fifty one from the Jammu region, four from Laddakh and six from outside the state.[16] Only five memoranda were from political parties, twelve emanated from various 'communal' bodies, of the rest, a little less than one-third were submitted by associations, unions and communities. The bulk of the remaining forty seven were from individuals, or group of individuals, whereas forty memoranda were essentially of general nature and dealt with the region and their problems. Other twenty eight had a 'communal bias' and related to protection and promotion of certain communal interests. After analysing the data and from the oral evidences recorded, the commission classified the grievances of the people in four major heads: (A) Development and Regional bias, (B) Employment, (C) Kashmir domination and (D) Education and discrimination and irritants responsible for rancour ill-will and animosity between the regions.[17]

Recommendations of Gagendra Gadkar Commission, 1968

The commission submitted its report on 6th December, 1968:

1. The commission recommeded for the establishment of two boards, one Statutory State Development Board and other Statutory Regional Development Board for three regions of Jammu, Kashmir and Laddakh. Regional Boards were under Chief Minister or Planning Minister and each board consisted of legislators from the regions, economic experts and concerned officials.[18]
2. The Commssion recommended that there should be recruitment rules for all the state services for which they do not exist. Suggestions were also made that Article 335 of The Constitution of India should be made applicable to Jammu and Kashmir state and reservation for the scheduled caste and backward classes be made in the services in proportion to their population. It should not exceed fifty per cent. The balance, if any, should be filled strictly and solely on the basis of merit.[19]
3. It also suggested that the government and the people of the state may themselves decide when Article 370 of The Constitution of India should be abrogated. The commission recommended that the state government should immediately take all steps to arrange for the holding of elections to the local bodies as early as possible. These elections should be held regularly in future.[20]
4. It also recommended that if the Chief Minister belongs to one region, there should be Deputy Chief Minister belonging to the other region. It also suggested that the number of Cabinet Minister belonging to the two region should be equal.[21]
5. It was recommended that when the High Court of Jammu and Kashmir functions at Srinagar, there should be at least one High Court Judge stationed at Jammu to dispose of the cases. Similarly, when

the High Court is functioning at Jammu, there should be at least one High Court Judge stationed at Srinagar to deal with the cases arising in Kashmir.[22]

6. It was recommended that some of the cadres should be district based, certain region based and the balance state based. In district based cadres transfers should be based permissible only within the district and in region based cadres transfers should be permissible only with in the region. It also recommended that the setting up of a Regional Recruitment Board for each of Jammu and Kashmir regions, and District Recruitment Board for each district in the state including Laddakh.[23]
7. It was also recommended that there should be a separate full fledged university in both the Jammu and Kashmir regions as all the professional colleges are located in Kashmir. It was recommended to open a new medical college in the Jammu region.[24]
8. The commission rejected the main demand of the Autonomy Forum, to provide a mechanism for effective sharing and decentralisation of political power among the regions. According to the commission, the large majority of the population in Jammu region did not support the proposal for regional autonomy regarding the question of regional imbalanced and Autonomy to Jammu region, the Gajendera Gadkar Commission was a mile stone. Although, it accepted that was discrimination and imbalance did exist, but it did not accept the demand for autonomy.[25]

In 1971, after the death of Mr Sadiq, Syed Mir Qasim became the Chief Minister of the state and remained in power for four years. As a chief minister, he enunciated the outlines of his programme for economic and social progress of the state, but he could not succeed in having a special control on the administration and the state politics especially in Jammu region.[26]

In 1971, however, the people of Jammu got another opportunity to launch a struggle against the norms prescribed by the Representation of People Act.

According to 1971 census, the population of Kashmir was 24,35,701 and that of Jammu at 20,75,640. But according to the third Jammu and Kashmir Delimitation Commission the people of Kashmir were given 42 seats in the legislative assembly at the rate of 37,992 persons per constituency, while the people of Jammu were to return 31 legislators at the rate of 66,956 persons per constituency.[27] This was enough to provoke a sort of furor for the people of Jammu to construct the recommendations of the Jammu Kashmir Delimitation Commission as an effort on their self respect[28] and also a slaught on democracy. The consequence of the protests in Jammu was that Sheikh Abdullah created an additional seat for its people by increasing the number of assembly seats from 75 to 76 in 1976. However, this gesture of Shiekh Abdullah could not conciliate the people of Jammu. As a matter of fact, they made it clear that they would continue their struggle till they obtained representation in the assembly in proportion of their population and few more seats on the basis of area, nature of terrain and state of communication system.[29] But the situation did not change.

Similarly, there was resentment in Jammu region over the number of districts in Jammu. Qadri Commission was appointed to examine the demands of the Jammu district and Kashmir district. Qadri Commission rejected out the right for the creation of new district either in Jammu region or in Kashmir division.[30]

Indira-Sheikh Accord, 1975

The year 1975 was a turning point in the history of Jamnu and Kashmir. In 1975, famous Indira-Sheikh Accord was signed and Sheikh Abdullah was installed as Chief Minister by Congress Government. When Sheikh Abdullah was in power, he did not do much with regard to regional autonomy.[31]

Sheikh Abdullah took steps which partially diminished the existing share of Jammu region in the state power structure. The state government diverted the central grants to Kashmir valley ignoring the claim of Jammu and Laddakh. It ate the share of these regions in the state services and admission to professional colleges. The state government filled up vacancies in different departments of Jammu province by people of Kashmir region. Not only this, the National Conference leadership mooted the idea of greater Kashmir, taking cue from Dixon plan. It proposed to create extended Kashmir by separate Muslim majority areas of Jammu province (Poonch, Rajouri, Doda and part of Udhampur district) and administratively linking it with Kashmir valley. This move was strongly opposed by all sections in Jammu, as they saw in it a attempt to divide Jammu province on communal lines.

On 30th June, 1977, the state assembly elections were held in which National Conference won 39 seats out of 42 in the valley seven out of 32 in Jammu region and both seats from Laddakh. National Conference lost 25 seats in Jammu because Jammu people were against the Sheikh Abdullah government.[32]

In early 1977, Lok Sabha elections were held. National Conference staged a strong come back through Sheikh Abdullah's election slogans –*"Majen yazath thra-hat-sathat, Bhanyan yazath thra-hat-sathat,*[33] *Bhayan yazath thra-hat-sathat."* This slogan was disliked by the national level leaders because in this slogan Skeikh Abdullah said,

'The respect of mothers, sisters and brothers are due to Article 370. Sheikh Abdullah laid more stress on special status and autonomy became a common feature during the election campaign. On 30 March, 1977, Congress decided to withdraw its support to Sheikh Abdullah's government.[34]

On 9th July, 1977, Sheikh Abdullah was sworn as the Chief Minister of Jammu and Kashmir state.[35] But still all the Jammu-based senior politicians reiterated almost every day that the discontent among the people of Jammu region has reached an explosive stage and that the impending disaster could be averted only with the acceptance of their demands which seeks the establishment of a democratically elected autonomous council invested with adequate political, administrative and financial power.[36]

With the establishment of a separate university, medical college and engineering college after 1977 in Jammu region helped to spread the politico-cultural activities and political consciousness in general. However, as subsequent events, like the Poonch agitation and the demands leading to the appointment of Sikri and Wazir commissions, proved the reference point to almost all political activities in Jammu. Jammu was under Kashmir politics which Jummuites could never accept with equanimity and which was signed by National Conference's return to power between 1975-1977.[37]

References

1. Jamwal Anajana Rani, Issues and *Aspirations in Jammu Region: A Political Profile,* Dissertation 1991, pp. 13-34.
2. Mahajan, Hari Om, Choudhary, Rekha, Jaghmohan, Published, Jay Kay Book House, Jammu, 1999, p. 91.
3. Singh, Karan, *Sadar-i-Riyst: An Autobiography,* Oxford University, New Delhi, 1985, p. 141.
4. Puri, Balraj, *Jammu and Kashmir Triumph and Tragedy of Indian Federalisation,* New Delhi, 1981, pp. 97-98.
5. *Ibid.*
6. In the opinion of Balraj Puri, the trouble lies in the non-recognition of Jammu as an entity. It is obvious that the recognition of Jammu as a separate political and constitutional entity would not find favour with those who count. They fear that such recognition would lead to separatist tendencies.
7. Puri, Balraj, op. cit., pp. 35-36.
8. *Gagendra Gadkar Commission Report,* 29th November, 1967, p. 14.
9. *Gajendra Gadkar Commission Report* 29th November, 1967, p. 14.
10. *Jammu's Discontent–causes and curses,* Memorandum submitted to Gajendra Gadkar Commission by Jammu Autonomy Forum Delhi. 1967, p. 6.
11. *Ibid.*
12. *Ibid.*
13. *Ibid.*
14. *Hindustan Times,* New Delhi, 29th November 1965, p. 7.
15. *Gajendra Gadkar Commission,* op. cit, p. 3.
16. *Ibid,* pp. 102-115.

17. *Ibid.*, p. 5.
18. *Ibid.*, p. 5.
19. *Ibid.*, p. 97.
20. *Ibid.*, p. 98.
21. *Ibid.*, p. 99.
22. *Ibid.*
23. *Ibid.*
24. *Ibid.*, p. 100
25. *Indian Express,* August 19th, 1967, p. 2.
26. Bafhzal, P.N.K., op. cit., pp. 819-20.
27. *Census of 1971*, p. 92.
28. Barnzai, P.N.K, op. cit., pp. 819-820.
29. Mahajan, Hariom, Anand, Hari, op. cit., p. 26.
30. *Ibid.*, pp. 42-44.
31. *The Kashmir Times,* August 8th, 1989, p. l.
32. *Indian Express,* 16th July, 1977, *Regional Autonomy–Theory and Background,* p. 5.
33. The Kashmir Times, Srinagar, 12 March, 1977, pp. 1-3.
34. *Ibid.*, 3 April 1977, p. l.
35. *Tribune*, 19th July, 1977, *Regional Autonomy,* p. 3.
36. Mahajan, Hari Om, op. cit., p. 45.
37. *For Jammu State Hood,* A phamphlet issued by Satya Pal, General Secretary Pardesh Lok Dal, p. l.

CONCLUSION

By political consciousness of the people one means a community's awareness of their collective interests and rights. It is acquired through a variety of ways, like the spread of education, newspapers, contacts with outsiders and the outside world, and *above all* by the feeling that they are being exploited and denied their right by the privileged and the powerful. Jammu and Kashmir was so situated on the map of India that it had relatively little contact with the outside world, except through the tourists who came to Kashmir and the shawl traders who went to the big cities of India. Even this contact was limited mostly to Kashmir where people went usually by the Jawahar Valley Road. Western education, too, was introduced here only by the end of the nineteenth century and the first college was established at Jammu in 1907. Here the first newspaper made its appearance much later. Certain administrative measures were initiated to modernise the living condition of the people, like the constitution of the Jammu Municipality. But on the whole, life moved in old channels in the old way, for the vast majority of the people of Jammu division. When the first public association was formed in 1904, known as the Dogra Sabha it was essentially a meeting place of the small but growing educated elite of Jammu, who demanded certain beneficial measures for the progress of the people as well as for the professional and economic benefit of the well-placed. Since the ruling family and most senior officials came from Jammu which was the seat of power, the average Jammuite had no visible reason to feel exploited. Their ethno-culture links with the ruler made them ignore and to accept the exploitations that the Kashmere Muslims were later to resent, because of the ethno-cultural divide that made them feel different and discriminated against. The Muslims of Jammu region, mostly Gujjars and Bakerwals, had their obvious sense of separate identity and interest, as different from Jammu Hindus. But, till very recent days, they were too backward educationally and economically to be heard or taken notice of. So, for all practical purposes, in the period between 1904 and 1977, political consciousness worth a study remained confined essentially to the upper caste urban non-Muslims in the three districts where they formed a majority.

However, even in the place life of Jammu some stirrings were caused by the first world war and the Bolshevik revolutions. People freely talked of the war and large number of Dogra soldiers went out, even abroad, to return home as literate and changed persons. The Russian revolution inspired new hopes in the hearts of many, who yearned for a just world and demanded more rights and responsibilities. In the changed condition the first newspaper of Jammu, the *Ranbir,* made its appearance in 1924. The elite of Jammu represented by the Dogra Sabha began clamouring for the protection of their interests and ambition and petitioned to the Maharaja to debar all outsiders from owning property in this state and taking up government jobs, so that their privileged position remained unchallenged. In response to the demand, the state subject law was passed by the Maharaja in 1927.

The educationally backward Kashmere Muslims, however, stood not to gain from this law and resented their virtual second class position in the twin fields of education and jobs. They resented what appeared to them as the discriminatory policy of the Dogra rulers of Jammu and began agitating for reforms on democratic lines. It was essentially in response to their agitation, leading to the bloody show down of 13th July, 1931 and the formation of Muslim Conference, that the Glancy Commission was appointed and in 1934, the Praja Sabha was constituted to aid and to advise the ruler. Unlike the Kashmere Muslims the Jammuites did not view the Praja Sabha as a weapon to wrest power and rights from the absolute ruler. They had every reason to be loyal and viewed with unease the growing Muslim demand for democratic right and for representation everywhere in proportion to their actual number. However, after the major segment of the Muslim Conference changed themselves into the National Conference in 1939, many in Jammu joined it out of an idealistic preference for the individual's rights and justice. But the National Conference could never become a major political force among the Hindus of Jammu, while Muslims here were too backward to effective political mobilisation.

The second world war and the August rebellion did stir the people of Jammu. Many went out to fight in Burma and south-east Asia, and returned with their eyes and ears open to the world around them. The threat to India poised by the advancing Japanese army and the Quit India movement that swept British India, did not leave the people of Jammu division untouched. Their most visible response was the *Roti* agitation of 1943 against the scarcity war, the Bengal famine, and other measures relating to the war had brought about. However, what agitated the people of Jammu division more was their reaction to the Quit Kashmir movement in the valley, which was viewed by the people here as an attack on the Dogra ruling house and, therefore, on the Dogra Hindus themselves. Scarcely had the state emerged out of the vortex of this agitation when it was overtaken by the storm that was unleashed by the prospects of immediate independence, partition, lapse of paramouncy and an unparalleled communal holocaust. Obviously, things were going to change soon and almost completely. Yet, initially both the Hindus and Muslims of Jammu, represented by the Rajya Hindu Sabha and the Muslim Conference, led by Hamidullah Chowdhary, were in favour of the continuance of the ruling dynasty and the maintenance of internal *status quo* of the state with an independent status. It was only when the blood bath of the neighbouring Punjab spilled over into this state that the Hindus and Muslims of Jammu began urging the Maharaja to accede to India and Pakistan, respectively. But even then, there was no significant movement here for the state's accession to either.

The situation, however, was suddenly changed beyond all expectations when, by the end of October 1947, the Pak raiders overwhelmed the state force and arrived within a striking distance of Srinagar. A Panic-sticken Maharaja had no option but to seek Indian help by acceding to her, which he did on 27.10.1947. But the accession also meant the institution of a popular government. Effective power was soon transferred to the National Conference representing the Kashmere Muslim elite, and the centre of political gravity of this state shifted forever from Jammu to Srinagar, from the upper caste Hindus to the Sunni Muslims of Kashmir. For the elite of Jammu, it was too severe a loss of power and status to bear with equanimity, especially when it was the Hindu-Sikh soldiers who had saved the valley. Moreover, the privileged Hindus resented the *Landed Estates Act* whereby all large agricultural estates, mostly owned by Rajputs and Kashmere Pandits, were confiscated without compensation, while the orchards, mostly owned by Kashmere Muslims, were exempted from the purview of this Act. The accumulated resentment of the elite of Jammu found its expression in the Praja Parishad agitation organised by Dina Nath Verma and Prem Nath Dogra, with the active support of the RSS, the

Hindu Maha Sabha, the Ram Rajya Parishad and later the Jana Sangh. However, the agitation too dependent on *zamindars* and *sahukars* and lacking in support from New Delhi fizzled out after a few years. However, the leaders of this movement and the Jammu non-Muslims in general, had the vicarious satisfaction of seeing their arch opponent Sheikh Abdullah bundled out of office into prison. His successors, especially Bakshi Ghulam Mohammad, kept the people of Jammu in humour with pro-India rhetoric and by doing out massive aid to ensure the material satisfaction of the people. Jammuites, by and large, forgot what they were missing in the mist of what they were receiving.

However, doles cannot deceive a people for too long and soon the Jammuites began resenting the discrimination they were being subjected to in two crucial matters, like employment and funds for development. Everywhere they were treated as the poor cousins of the Kashmere Muslims. So, many now raised the demand for reservations or regional autonomy to ensure genuine self-rule and justice. It was Jammu's demand for a probe into regional imbalance that led to the appointment of the Gajendra Gadkar Commission, in 1967. Some of its recommendations were accepted, while many were ignored and Jammu's resentment continued to grow. They resented both the exploitative power the Kashmeres enjoyed their anti-Indian attitude. These ensured that the Hindus of Jammu gradually acquired a communal bent of mind, which is not just anti-Kashmir, but also anti-Muslim. Urban Jammuites mostly became staunch supporters of the Jan Sangh/ BJP point of view, while in the countryside the Hindus and Muslims usually voted for the Congress and the National Conference, respectively, except, of course, during the elections of 1977, because of the nationwide anti-

Congress polarisation, Jammu people, by and large, voted for the Janta Party.

In the meantime, however, in line with the broad recommendations of the Gajendra Gadkar Committee, a little more attention had come to be focussed on Jammu, where a separate university was formed, and within a few years, Jammu had her own medical and engineering colleges, as well. These naturally helped the spread of politico-cultural activities and of political consciousness, in general. However, as subsequent events, like the Poonch agitation and the demands leading to the appointment of the Sikri and Wazir Commissions, proved the reference point for almost all political activity in Jammu. It remained Kashmere dominance, which the Jammuites could never accept with equanimity and which was signalled by the National Conference return to power, between since 1975 to 1977.

BIBLIOGRAPHY

A. Primary Sources

Archives-unpublished records

a. Indian National Archive Home and Foreign Deptt.

- *File No. 9 of 1910.*
- *File No. 526 of 1911.*
- *File No. 57/59 of 1917.*
- *File No. 30 of 1917.*
- *File No. 28 of 1917.*
- *File No. 39 of 1918.*
- *File No. 388/404 of 1918.*
- *File No. M 175 of 1918.*
- *File No. 14/33 of 1919.*
- *File No.9 of 1919.*
- *File No. 48 of 1919.*
- *File No. 18 of 1921.*
- *File No. 199 of 1921.*
- *File No. 22/38 of 1921.*
- *File No. 18 of 1922.*
- *File No. 19 of 1923.*
- *File No. 39 of 1927.*
- *File No. 18 of 1931.*
- *File No. 423 of 1931.*
- *File No. 21 of 1939 .*

- *File No. 67/Part-II of 1946.*
- *File No. 59 of 1953 .*
- *File No. 39 of 1954 b.*

(b) State Govt. Records:

- *File No. 13/4 of 1904.*
- *File No. 117/p. 51 of 1904.*
- *File No. 46-5-18 of 1904.*
- *File No. 40-5-18 of 1904.*
- *File No. 62 of 1904.*
- *File No. 131 of 1905.*
- *File No. 205/M-144 of 1906.*
- *File No. 30/1 of 1906.*
- *File No. 51/1-71 of 1906.*
- *File No. 164 of 1906.*
- *File No. 149 of 1906.*
- *File No. 99/N-102 of 1907.*
- *File No. 280 of 1909.*
- *File No. 43 of 1909.*
- *File No. 71/N/13/2 of1909.*
- *File No. ISO/Part-II of 1910.*
- *File No. 202/N-51 C of 1910.*
- *File No. 215 of 1910.*
- *File No. 49/P-33 of 1911.*
- *File No. 157/C of1911.*
- *File No. 162 of 1912.*
- *File No. 238/P-47 of1912.*
- *File No. 34 of 1912.*
- *File No. 254/P. 127 of1912.*
- *File No. 242/P. 38 of 1912.*
- *File No. 27/45-C of 1913.*
- *File No. 418/PS-49 of 1913.*
- *File No. 91/P. 56 of1913.*

- *File No. 69/2-106 of 1913.*
- *File No. 213/P. 106 of1913.*
- *File No. 58/6-34 of 1913.*
- *File No.221/F-116 of1913.*
- *File No. 204/2-159 of 1914.*
- *File No. 71 of 1914.*
- *File No.33-9/C of1914.*
- *File No. 57/38-C of 1916.*
- *File No.25/45-C of 1917.*
- *File No. 27/43-C of 1917.*
- *File No. 215 of 1917.*
- *File No.61/P. 307 of1917.*
- *File No. 264/23 of 1917.*
- *File No.234/P. 53 of1917.*
- *File No. 261/28 of 1917.*
- *File No.21/28-C of1917.*
- *File No. 27/43-C of 1917.*
- *File No.61/P. 307 of 1918.*
- *File No. 262/77-C of 1918.*
- *File No.216/P. 92 of1918.*
- *File No.213-P. 68 of 1918.*
- *File No. 23/31-C of 1919.*
- *File No. 125/40 of 1919.*
- *File No. 10/327 of 1919.*
- *File No.312/2-C of1919.*
- *File No. 126/16 N-C of 1919.*
- *File No.70/Jud.Of 1919.*
- *File No. 72/JLE of 1919.*
- *File No.69/N-Eof 1919.*
- *File No. 39/2 of 1919.*
- *File No. 265/129 of 1920.*
- *File No. 225/129 of 1920.*

- *File No. 229 of 1920.*
- *File No. 209 of 45-C of 1920.*
- *File No. 99/C-l of 1920.*
- *File No.216/C-37of 1920.*
- *File No.200/Cofl920.*
- *File NO.104/1-C of 1920.*
- *File No.354/Cofl920.*
- *File No. 121 of 1920.*
- *File No. 162 of 1921.*
- *File No. 157 of 1921.*
- *File No.63/60-Cofl921.*
- *File No. 254/C of 1921.*
- *File No. 180 of 1921.*
- *File No.73/97-Cofl921.*
- *File No. 261/28 of 1921.*
- *File No. 162 of 1922.*
- *File No. 55 of 1922.*
- *File No.386/P. 33 of 1923.*
- *File No.267/P. 57 of 1923.*
- *File No.396-M of 1923.*
- *File No. 72/JLF of 1924.*
- *File No.97/63-g of 1924.*
- *File No.93/63-g of 1924.*
- *File No. 334 of 1925.*
- *File No. 217 of 1925.*
- *File No.57/38-C of 1926.*
- *File No. J-31 of 1927.*
- *File No. 259/5-32 of 1930.*
- *File No. 326 of 1930.*
- *File No. 417/5-23 of 1931.*
- *File No. 13/23 of 1931.*
- *File No.418/PS-149 of 1931.*

- *File No. 13/14 of 1931.*
- *File No. 261/5-2 of 1931.*
- *File No. 327 of 1931.*
- *File No. 12 of 1931.*
- *File No. 18 of 1931.*
- *File No. 138/2 of 1931.*
- *File No. 167/29 of 1931.*
- *File No. 18 of 1931.*
- *File No. 423 of 1931.*
- *File No. 479 of 1931.*
- *File No. 485 of 1931.*
- *File No. 474 of 1931.*
- *File No. 80/10-G of 1931.*
- *File No. 93/10 of 1931.*
- *File No. 86/104 of 1931.*
- *File No. 84 of 1931.*
- *File No. 167/129 of 1931.*
- *File No.PS-298/12 of 1931.*
- *File No. 94 of 1932.*
- *File No. 134/ 43 of 1932.*
- *File No. 156/ 8-5 of 1932.*
- *File No. 92 of 1932.*
- *File No. 90/39 of 1932.*
- *File No. 99 of 1932.*
- *File No. 190/ 292 of 1932.*
- *File No. 416/72 of 1932.*
- *File No. 194/104 of 1932.*
- *File No. 208/217 of 1932.*
- *File No. 297/88 of 1932.*
- *File No. 667IPS-579 of 1932.*
- *File N0.232II-PAS of 1932.*
- *File No. 109 of 1932.*

- *File No 94 of 1932.*
- *File No. 200 1194 of 1932.*
- *File No. 1921PS-169 of 1932.*
- *File No. 298 of 1932.*
- *File No. 402123 of 1932.*
- *File No. 420 of 1932.*
- *File No. 422 of 1932.*
- *File No. 267IP. 579 of 1932.*
- *File No. 390144 of 1932.*
- *File No. 418182 of 1932.*
- *File No. 4871PS-88 of 1932.*
- *File No. 2081217 of 1932.*
- *File No. PS-1901292 of 1932.*
- *File No. 1351 P. 5 of 1932.*
- *File No. 59 of 1933.*
- *File No. 481 / PS-49 of 1933.*
- *File No. 13/ 10-A of 1934.*
- *File No. 51/1-27 of 1936.*
- *File No. 41 /p. J 5 of J 937.*
- *File No. 31/D-6 of 1937.*
- *File No. 174/D-37 of 1937.*
- *File No. 44/D-15 of 1937.*
- *File No. 128/B-446/38of 1938.*
- *File No. 129 /B-44 of 1938.*
- *File No. 390 of 1938.*

(c) Govt Unpublished Records

1. His Highness Messages to His Believed People 9th July, 1931.
2. Stormy demonstrations in Jammu, *Kashmir Bureau of Information,* New Delhi.
3. *Jammu and Kashmir Constituent Assembly opening address by Hon'ble S.M. Abdullah,* Srinagar.

November 3rd, 1951, printed at Caxton Press, New Delhi.

4. *Revised List* of Ruling Princes Chief and leading personage of the L & K State of Gilgit Agencies.
5. Unanimous Vote of Confidence in Bakshi Government *Ranbir* Govt., Press, Jammu.
6. The Flag Issue by *Kashmir Bureau of Information,* New Delhi.
7. *India and Kashmir* (Constitutional Aspect).
8. Kashmir Appeal to World Conscience by S.M. Abdullah, Ranbir Press.
9. *Kashmir – A Glorious Valley* by J.L. Nehru, 1939, New Delhi.
10. Jammu situation an objective analysis by S.M. Abdullah by *Ranbir Press.*
11. *Report Book-On the Road of New Kashmir,* New Delhi.
12. *Sir Ganga Ram Report,* State Archive Repository, Jammu.
13. *Report by L.W. Jardine,* LCS, Special Minister on the measures adopted for the restoration of law and order in Mirpur Wazarat and Rajouri Tehsil.
14. *Report on an inquiry into disturbance at Jammu and its environment* during first week of November 1931 conducted by L. Middleton LCS.
15. His Highness Govt Jammu and Kashmir – *Orders* on the Recommendations Contained III the Glancy Commission's Report.
16. *Report of the Commission* appointed under the orders of His Highness the Maharaja Bahadur dated the 12th November 1931 to enquire into grievances and complaints.
17. *His Highness Govt Jammu and Kashmir Evidence Recorded in Republic* by the Srinagar Riots Enquiry Committee.

18. *Documents* relating to Poonch State Archive Jammu.
19. *Report* - Five months issued by Directorate of Information and Broadcasting, Jammu and Kashmir state.
20. A note on Jammu and Kashmir State - 1928, *Ranbir Press*, Jammu.
21. *Report - Kashmir Averts National Disaste* (Bakshi Gulam Mohammad Call to People).
22. *A Report – Jammu and Kashmir Regional Autonomy,* Mehra off-set Press, New Delhi.
23. Sadar-i-Riyst, *Address to Legislative Assembly.* Jammu, 24 March, 1954.

(d) Hand Books

1. *A Hand Book of J&K State.* Govt Publications, Ranbir Govt Press.
2. *A Hand Book of J&K Govt* J&K Administrative Reports, Ranbir Press, 1945.
3. *A Hand Book – Jammu and Kashmir Operations 1947-48,* Questions and Answers, Himalayan Books, New Delhi.
4. *A Hand Book of J&K State, 1947-1959,* An account of activities of first three years of Sheikh Abdullah's Govt. Printed at Ranbir Press, Jammu 1951.
5. *A Hand Book of J&K State,* Jammu situation (an objective analysis) Published by Kashmir Bureau of Information, New Delhi and Printed at Caxton Press, New Delhi.
6. *A Hand Book of J&K State Praja Parishad Movement in Jammu,* A STAB in India's Back by Piyar Singh by National Publishing House, Jammu.

(e) Administration Reports

1. A. R. Year 1930-31.

A. R. Year 1932-33.

A. R. Year 1933-35.
A. R. Year 1936-37.
A. R. Year 1939-40.
A. R. Year 1941-43.
A. R. Year 1943-44.
A. R. Year 1944-45.
A. R. Year 1946-49.
A. R. Year 1949-50.
A. R. Year 1951-52.
A. R. Year 1952-53.
A. R. Year 1953-54.
A. R. Year 1954-55.
A. R. Year 1955-56.
2. Part-II. 26th March to 8th April, 1936.
3. Vol. V, Part-I Sixth to 17 Oct. 1936, 5 session.
4. Vol. VI, 6th April, 1937, Sixth session.
5. Vol. VI, Part-V, 14th April, 1937, Sixth session.
6. Vol. VI, Part-X, 22nd April, 1937, Sixth session.
7. Vol. VI, Part-XI, 22nd April, 1937, Sixth session.
8. Vol. VI, Part-XII, 27th April, 1937, Sixth session.
9. Vol. VI, Part-XV, 29th April, 1937, Sixth session.

(g) Assembly Debates

Vol. I, II, III of 1935.
Vol. IV of 1936 Part-I.
Vol. IV of 1936 Part-II.
Vol. VI of 1937.

(h) Commission Reports

1. *Report of the Jammu and Kashmir Commission of Inquiry (1967).*
2. *Report of the Jammu and Kashmir Commission of Inquiry (1972).*

3. *Annual Bulletin of Vital Statistics* Govt. of Jammu and Kashmir, 1987.

(i) **Pamphlets**

1. *Plea for State Subject, Definition and Genesis,* by Dogra Sadhar Sabha.
2. *Article 370 and Regional Autonomy,* Balraj Puri, (Jammu N.D).
3. *One Day Convention of Jammu Maha Sabha: A Report,* Jammu Mahasabha (Jammu N.D).
4. *A Ringing Call for Sanity Goodwill and Communal Unity Jammu,* Maha Sabha (Jammu N.D).
5. *Jammu Discontent – Causes and Cures,* Balraj Puri, Delhi, 1967.
6. *Birth Pangs of New Kashmir* By N.S. Phalke, Published by Ranbir Press.

(j) **Census Reports**

1. *Census 1911, K, Part-I Vol. XX.*
2. *Census 1921, K, Part-I, Vol. XXII.*
3. *Census 1921, K, Part-I and II, Vol. XXIV.*
4. *Census of India, 1931, J&K State, Part-I.*
5. *Census 1931, J&K, Part-II.*
6. *Census of India 1941, J&K State, Part-I and II.*

(k) **Manuscripts**

1. Wazir Ganga Nath, "A Report on the Administration of Jammu and Kashmir State", 1942, Jammu Archieve.

(l) **Journals:**

1. Bharatiya Jana – Sangh 'Kashmir Problem and Jammu Satyagraha, an Objective Study'. New Delhi (N.D.).

(m) Letters:

Pt Prem Nath Dogra's Letter to the Minister of Revenue and Agriculture, Govt of Jammu and Kashmir, 9th April, 1932, Available from family sources.

B. Secondary Sources

(a) Articles

1. Facing Internal Threats to nations integrity, www.Hindu.Book/Org/Vision.
2. Dhar, Trilokinath A story of Kashmir Affair–A keep into the past, *Kashmir Samachar,* Articles on Politics.
3. Bhasin, Yash, Pt Prem Nath Dogra: A man of Commitment and conviction, *Daily Excelssior,* (N.D.).
4. Dogra Durga Dass, Pt Prem Nath Dogra, *Panorama,* Jammu
5. Socio-Religious Activities of the Arya Samaj and Kashmir state, *Maharshi Dayanand University Research Journal (Acts),* Vol. 3, Numbers, 1988, p. 43.

(f) Praja Sabha Debates

1. *Vol. IV, Part-I, 16th to 25th March, 1936, 4th session.*

(b) Newspapers:

1. *Chand* in Urdu (1940-1961).
2. *Ranbir* in Urdu (1919-1952).
3. *The Dogra Gazette* in Urdu (1932-1953).
4. *Khalid,* Srinagar.
5. *Martand,* Srinagar.
6. *Hamdard,* Srinagar.
7. *Kidmat,* Srinagar.

8. *Tribune,* Srinagar.
9. *Statesman,* Srinagar.
10. *Ranbir,* Weekly, Jammu.
11. *Daily Excelsior.*
12. *The Kashmir Times.*
13. *Hindustan Times.*
14. *The Times of India.*
15. *Indian Express.*
16. *Forum/Bombay.*
17. *Kashmir Samachar.*
18. *Panorama.*

(c) Magazines

Janata, Vol. XXII, March 1978.

(d) Interview:

1. B.P. Sharma.
2. O.P. Shastri.

(e) Thesis and Dissertations

1. Bharham, K., *Political Agitation in Kashmir in 1931 and emergence of Muslim Conference,* Dissertation, History Deptt., Jammu.
2. Kumar, Sudarshan, *Social History of Jammu City, From 1885 to 1947 A.D.,* Dissertation, History Deptt., Jammu.
3. Ganesh, Gosawmi, *Beggar System in Jammu and Kashmir,* Dissertation, History Deptt., Jammu.
4. Edison, David1982, *'Sher-i-Kashmir: A lion of Kashmir, Sheikh Abdullah and Dispute over relationship between J&K State and the Indian Union,* University Microfilms, International Annarbour Michigan U.S.A., London, thesis.

5. Gupta, Kishore Lal, *Social History of Jammu Province from 1901-1961,*. Thesis, 1984, History Deptt,. Jammu.
6. Bala, Renu, *Regional Political Parties and Constitutional Developments of Jammu and Kashmir – A Study of Praja Parishad* – 1999. Dissertation, Pol. Science Deptt., Jammu.
7. Jamwal, Anjana Rani, *Issue and aspiration in Jammu region: A Political Profile 1999,* Dissertation, Political Science Deptt., Jammu.
8. Kapoor, M.L., *Social, Economic History of Jammu and Kashmir State, 1885-1925,* Thesis, History Deptt., Jammu.

(f) Books

1. Anand, A.S., *The constitution of Jammu and Kashmir: Its Development and Contents,* Second edition and third edition, Delhi Universal Law Publishing, New Delhi. 1994, 1998.
2. Anand, A.S., *The Development of Constitution of Jammu and Kashmir,* Light and Life Publishers, New Delhi, 1980.
3. Andrew and Mukerjee, *Rise and Growth of Congress in India,* Meenakshi Prakashan, Meerut, 1967.
4. Aggarwal, J.C., S.P., *Modern History of Jammu and Kashmir Vol. I and II Ancient Times to Shimla Agreement,* New Delhi, 1995.
5. Akbar, M.I. *India – The Seige, Penguin,* New Delhi, 1985.
6. Bazaz, P.N., *Struggle for Freedom in Kashmir,* Kashmir Publishing, Srinagar, 1954.
7. Bazaz, P.N., *Inside Kashmir,* Kashmir Publishing, Srinagar, 1951.
8. Bamzai, P.N.K., *A History of Kashmir,* Metropolitan, New Delhi, 1966.

9. Bamzai, P.N.K., *A History of Kashmir – Political, Social and Cultural from the Earliest to the present date,* New Delhi, 1962.
10. Bamzai, P.N.K., *Cultural and Political History of Kashmir,* Vol. 3, *Modern Kashmir*, D. Publications, 1994.
11. Bhat, Koul, Ram Krishan, *Political and Constitutional Development of the Jammu and Kashmir* Seema Publications, New Delhi, 1989.
12. Bhattacharjea, Ajit, *Kashmir– The Wounded Valley,* UBS Publishers and Distributors Ltd., New Delhi, 1994.
13. Bose, Sumantra, *The Challenge in Kashmir – Democracy Self Determination and a Just Peace,* Sage Publication, New Delhi, 1997.
14. Bakshi, S.R., *Sheikh Mohammad Abdullah,* Book House, Jammu, 1995.
15. Bushan, D.R., Vidhy, *State Politics and Govt Jammu and Kashmir,* House, Jammu, 1964.
16. Biscoe, C.E., Tyndali – *Kashmir in see light and Shade,* London, 1922.
17. Charak, Sukhdev Singh, *History and Culture of Himalayan States – Jammu and Kashmir,* Light and Life, New Delhi, 1983.
18. Chohan, Amar Singh, *Development of Education in the Jammu and Kashmir State,* Atlantic Publishers and Distributors, New Delhi, 2001.
19. Charak, Sukhdev Singh, *Histography of Jammu,* Book House, Jammu, 1997.
20. Das, Durga, *Sardar Patel's Correspondence, 1945-50,* Vol.1, Nov Jivan Publishing House Ahmedabad, 1971.
21. Dhar, Trilokinath, *History of Kashmir – A key into the past, Kashmir Samachar, Article in politics in*

Kashmir, Kashmir Information Com./Kash-Sam Kashmir Affairs, 2002.

22. Fazili, Manzoor, *Socialist Ideas and Movements in Kashmir, 1919-1947,* Gulshan Publication, Srinagar, 1982.
23. Gupta, Sisar, *Kashmir – A Study of India-Pakistan Relations,* Ana Publishing House, Bombay, 1956.
24. Hussain, Majid, *Geography of Jammu and Kashmir,* Rajesh Publications, New Delhi, 1987.
25. Hasnin, N., *Hindu, Muslim Relation,* A Publishing Corporation, New Delhi, 1996.
26. Handa, R.L., *Freedom Struggle in Princely State,* New Delhi, 1989.
27. Koul, Santosh, *Freedom Struggle in Jammu and Kashmir,* Anmol Publications, New Delhi, 1990.
28. Koul, Pt Anand, *Geography of Jammu and Kashmir State,* Life Publishers, New Delhi, 1978.
29. Khan G.H., *Freedom Struggle in Kashmir 1931-1940,* Light and Life Publishers, New Delhi, 1980.
30. Koul, Kachru, Shyam, Omkar, *Jammu, Kashmir and Ladakh Ringside Views,* Shyog Prakashan, New Delhi, 1998.
31. Kapur, M.L., *Maharaja Hari Singh, 1895-1961,* Har Anand Publications, Delhi, 1989.
32. Kour, Ravinderjeet, *Political Awakening in Kashmir,* APH Publishing Corporation, New Delhi, 1992.
33. Koul, G.L., *Kashmir Then and Now – A Historical Survey,* Publishing House, Srinagar, 1969.
34. Koul, Bhatt, Prem Krishan, *Political and Constitutional Development of Jammu and Kashmir,* Seema Publications, Delhi, 1990.
35. Kapur, M.L., *History of Jammu and Kashmir state,* Kashmir History Publications, Jammu, 1990.

36. Koul, S.N., *Dynamics of Kashmir Politics,* Ranjit Publications, New Delhi, 2001.
37. Kak, B.L., *Kashmir Problems and Politics,* Seema Publications, Delhi, 1981.
38. Kamble, J.R., *Rise and Awakening of Depressed Classes in India,* New Delhi, 1979.
39. Lamb, Alastair, *Arisen in Kashmir,* Delhi, 1967.
40. Modhok, Balraj, *Bungling in Kashmir,* New Delhi, 1974.
41. Modhok Balraj, *Kashmir Centre of New Alignments,* Deepak Prakashan, New Delhi, 1963.
42. Modhok, Balraj, *Jammu Kashmir Ladakh Problem and Solution,* Reliance Publishing House, New Delhi, 1987.
43. Mahajan, Hari Om, *A study in the spread of Education and Consciousness, 1857-1925,* New Delhi, 1980.
44. Mahajan, Hari Om, *Beyond the Kashmir Valley,* Har Anand Publications, New Delhi, 1998.
45. Mujumdar, R.C., *History of Freedom Movement in India,* Vol. III, Delhi, 1969.
46. Naqash, Shah, Nasir A., G.M., *Kashmir from Crises to Crises,* ADM Publishing Corporation, New Delhi. 1997.
47. Puri, Balraj, *Simmering Valcano: A Study of Jammu's Relation with Kashmir,* Sterling, New Delhi, 1981.
48. Puri, Balraj, *Jammu – A dice to Kashmir – angle,* New Delhi, 1966.
49. Puri, Balraj, *Jammu and Kashmir Triumph and Tragedy of Indian Federalisation,* Sterling, New Delhi, 1981.
50. Pannnikar, K.M., *Foundation of Kashmir State,* London, 1930.

51. Philips, C.H., *Evolution of India and Pakistan Documents,* New Delhi, 1991.

52. Raghvan, G.S., *The Warning in Kashmir,* Jay Kay Book House, Jammu, 1993.

53. Raghvan, G.S., *The Working of Kashmir,* Pioneer Press, Allahabad, 1931.

54. Risky, Scitterbert, *The People of India,* London, 1908.

55. Rai, Lajpat, *A History of Arya Samaj, An Account of its origin, doctrines and activities with a biographical sketch of account of its origin,* Calcutta, 1967.

56. Sharp, M., *A note on education in the state of Jammu and Kashmir,* Calcutta, 1916.

57. Singh, Karan, Sadar-i-Riyst: *An Autobiography,* Vol. 2, 1953-67, Oxford University Papers, New Delhi, 1985.

58. Singh, Karan, *Sadar-i-Riyst: An Autobiography,* Oxford University Press, New Delhi, 1982.

59. Saraf Muhammad Yusaf, *Kashmir's Fight for Freedom,* Vol. 12,1931-46,1947-48, Kashmir History Committee Edition, Lahore, 1977,1979.

60. Singh, Lt Co. Bhagwan, *Political Conspiracies of Kashmir,* Light and Life Publishers, New Delhi, 1973.

61. Shastri, R.N., *Dogra Deya Char Namvar Shaksayat* Dogri Sanstha, Jammu, 1969.

62. Shah, Gulshan, *State Subjectship in Jammu and Kashmir,* Mis Jupitor, Srinagar, 1938.

63. Sexana, H.L., *Tragedy of Kashmir,* Nationalist Publishers, New Delhi, 1975.

64. Saraf, M.R., *Jeewan Chariter, Sher-i-Dugar, Lala Hansraj, 1886-1944,* Jammu, 1907.

65. Saraf, M.R., *Fifty Years as a Journalist,* New Delhi, 1947.

66. Singh, Justice Jaswant, *Jammu and Kashmir Political and Constitutional Development,* Har Anand Publications, 1996.
67. Singh, Maj K. Brahma, Retd, *History of Jammu International,* New Delhi, 1990.
68. Singh, Narinder, *Political Awakening in Kashmir,* M.K. Publishers, Delhi, 1989.
69. Shahdari, Naveen, *The Arya Samaj Hindu without,* Hinduism, Vikas Publishing House, Delhi, 1972.
70. Singh, Nirmal Kumar, *Inter-Communal Relations in Jammu and Kashmir,* Book House, Jammu, 1989.
71. Sharma, S.P., *Heritage of Jammu and Kashmir and Ladakh,* Radha Publications, New Delhi, 2001.
72. Sharma, S.P., *Heritage of Jammu and Kashmir and Ladakh,* Radha Publications, New Delhi, 2001.
73. Saraf, Mulk Raj, *Shar-a-Dogra-Lala Hans Raj, 1866-1947,* Raj Mehal Publishers, Jammu, 1984.
74. Schofield, Victoria, *Kashmir in the Crossfire,* Published Vinod Vasistha for Viva Books, 1997.
75. Teng, M.K., State *Government and Political Jammu and Kashmir,* Anmol Publications, New Delhi, 1998.
76. Teng, M.K., *Kashmir Myth of Autonomy,* Anmol Publications, New Delhi, 1998.
77. Thakur, K.T. Harigh, *Alienation and Integration in Jammu and Kashmir,* Jaipur, 1999.
78. Teng, Koul, Mohan, Krishan, Santosh, *Kashmir's Special Status,* Oriental Publishers, Delhi, 1975.
79. Teng, Koul, Ram Krishan, *Kashmir Constitutional History and Documents,* New Delhi, 1977.
80. Teng, Mohan Krishan, *Kashmir Article 370,* Anmol Publications, New Delhi, 2001.

81. Vaid, Dr S.P., *How Partition Rocked Jammu and Kashmir,* Shyama Publications, Jammu, 2002.

82. Verma, P.S., *Jammu and Kashmir,* the Publishing House, New Delhi, 1994.

83. Vidya Bhushan – *State Politics and Government in Jammu and Kashmir,* Book House, Jammu, 1985.

84. Yassian, Mohammad, *History of Freedom Struggle in Jammu and Kashmir,* Life and Light Publishers, New Delhi, 1980.

85. Wadhwa, Dr K.K., *Constitutional Autonomy – A case study of J&K*, Bhavana Books and Prints, New Delhi, 1993.

86. Zutshi, U.K., *Emergence of Political Awakening in Kashmir,* New Delhi, 1986.

APPENDICES

NAME OF THE BODIES/ASSOCIATIONSI‘INDIVIDUALS WHO SUBMITTED WRITTEN MEMORANDUMS TO THE COMMISSION IN 1967-1968

Shri Abdul Aziz Shawl, Ex-MLA, P.O. Rajouri

All J&K Backward Classes Union, Jammu

All J &K Christian Association, Jammu

All J&K National Integration Front, Jammu

Anjuman Islamia, Jammu

Shri Bansi Lal Kohistani, Jammu

Beopar Mandal, Jammu

Bharatiya Depressed Classes League, Jammu

Congress Committee, Rajouri

District National Congress Committee, Udhampur

Dogra Mandal, Jammu

Dogra United Front, Jammu

Ex-Officers of the J&K Forces who retired before 1957, Jammu

Ex-Servicemen of J&K State, Jammu

Sofi Ghulam Ahmed Gash, Srinagar

Gujar Samaj Sudhar Sabha, Poonch District

Jammu Autonomy Forum

Jammu Citizen's Council, Jammu

Janta Adhikar Raksha Samiti, Jammu

J&K Agriculturists Association, Jammu.

Jammu and Kashmir Ravidas, Sabha, Jammu

J&K Shia United Front, Srinagar

Jammu and Kashmir State Gujar Samaj Sudhar Sabha, Jammu, Jammu and Kashmir Students Congress (Shri K. Sharma)

Jammu and Kashmir Students Congress (Shri Preetam Singh)

Shri J.R. Sethi of Jammu

Jat Sudhar Sabha, J&K State, Jammu

S/Shri Jivan Ram and Chabital Kapoor of Village Chakcharat

Ram, Baramullah.

Shri Khurshi Anwar Dogra, Jammu

Kisan Conference Doda, Jammu

Shri Mela Ram, Advocate, Jammu

Shri Mohan Lal Motial, Jammu

Shri Mulk Raj Acharya, Jammu

Nehru Ekata Committee, Jammu

Praja Socialist Party, Jammu and Kashmir State, Jammu

Secretary, Naya Bhawan, Jammu

Shri Guru Singh Sabha Jammu, Akali Dal Jammu Province

"Uprooted Muslims of Tehsil Ramnagar, District Udhampur

(Jammu)"

Zamindara Association, Jammu;

Anjuman Islamia, Jammu

Beopar Mandal, Jammu Dogra Mandal, Jammu

Dogra United Front, Jammu,

Ex-J&K Militia Personnel, Jammu,

Ex-serviceman of J&K State, Jammu

J&K Agriculturists Association, Jammu,

Janta Adhikar Raksha Samiti, Jammu,

Jat Sudhar Sabha, J&K State, Jammu,

Pradesh Congress Refugee Advisory Committee, Jammu,

Shri Guru Singh Sabha Jammu, Akali Dal Jammu Province, and Sikh Minority Board, Jammu and Kashmir, Jammu,

Sharnarthi Action Committee, Jammu, Sharnarthi Pratinidhi Board, Jammu,

Zamindara Association, Jammu

The Jammu and Kashmir State Gujar Samaj Sudhar Sabha

Jammu

Shri Guru Singh Sabha, Jammu and Kashmir, The Sikh Minority

Board

Sikh Riyasati Akali Dal, Jammu

Zamindara Association, Jammu

Agriculturists Association, Jammu

Janta Adhikar Raksha Samiti, Jammu

Anjuman Islamia, Jammu

Jammu Citizens Council, Jammu

Praia Socialist Party, Jammu and Kashmir State, Jammu

Shri Phulel Singh, Doda.

All J&K National Integration Front, Jammu.

All J&K Backward Classes Union, Jammu

J&K Ravidas Sabha, Jammu

Shri Prabhu Shoor, Village Kangri, Distt. Rajouri

Jat Sudhar Sabha, Jammu and Kashmir State, Jammu

All J&K Kshatriya Sadar Sabha, Jammu

Dogra Kashtriya Sadar Sabha, Jammu

Khukhran Bradri (Kashatriya Khukhran), Jammu

Beopar Mandal, Jammu

Convener, Pradesh Congress Refugee Advisory Committee,
Jammu

Chairman, Public Service Commission, Jammu

Chief Secretary: Commission, Planning and Development, Jammu

Finance Secretary: Food Commissioner; Revenue Secretary
Jammu

Additional Secretary, Education, Jammu

Shri G. L. Dogra, Minister of Revenue

Tribute to the Students

Martyrs of 17th and 18th October, 1966.

In the Loving Memory of the Students killed on 17th and 18th October, 1966.

Index

J